Ministry of Culture, Government of the State of São Paulo, through the Secretariat of Culture, Creative Economy and Industry, Municipal Secretariat of Culture and Creative Economy of the City of São Paulo, Fundação Bienal de São Paulo and Itaú present

Not All Travellers Walk Roads

36th Bienal de São Paulo

bienal

Of Humanity as Practice

Browse our YouTube channel and check out the documentation of the *Invocation #3*.

**Educational
Publication**

Vol. 3

Mawali–Taqsim:

Improvisation as a Space and Technology of Humanity

Since 1953, the year of its second edition, the Bienal de São Paulo has stood out for its educational commitment, promoting initiatives that facilitate access to exhibition content for diverse audiences – including teachers, students, and educators. In 2009, the Fundação Bienal established a permanent education team that has since been developing and implementing educational projects for each edition. These projects include publications, guided visits, workshops, and training programs for teachers and educators, all aimed at fulfilling the Fundação Bienal's mission of expanding access to contemporary art.

For the 36th Bienal de São Paulo – *Not All Travellers Walk Roads – Of Humanity as Practice*, the Fundação presents a series of four educational publications with two complementary objectives, both of fundamental importance to the Bienal. The first is to document and share the contributions of the *Invocations* – curatorial gatherings with artists and poets that explore notions of humanity, the exhibition's central theme, through the lens of four distinct geographies: Marrakech, Guadeloupe, Zanzibar, and Tokyo. The second objective is to support the educational project of the 36th Bienal, with these books serving as key resources in the training of mediators and in outreach activities, both during the months of preparation and execution of the exhibition and throughout the traveling exhibitions program that will follow.

As is characteristic of the Bienal de São Paulo, the content of these publications weaves together local and global perspectives, addressing contemporary practices and issues. The result of a partnership with the Center for Art, Research and Alliances (CARA), which co-published the books with the Fundação Bienal, and the A&L Berg Foundation, which supported the project from the outset, these educational publications are now available in English and will be distributed internationally for the first time, expanding the reach of the *Invocations* and our educational content, and reaffirming the Bienal's international vocation, which has been continuously enacted for over seventy years.

Andrea Pinheiro
President – Fundação Bienal de São Paulo

CARA is thrilled to co-produce this publication with the Bienal de São Paulo, reinforcing our shared commitment to expanding spaces for artistic and intellectual inquiry. The *Invocations* programs and these four educational volumes echo CARA's dedication to publishing as an act of transformation – where knowledge is not just recorded but activated through encounters across disciplines and geographies. Our institutional approach fosters open-ended research, challenges fixed narratives, and embraces storytelling as a means of keeping ideas in motion, unsettling dominant histories, and opening pathways for unlearning.

Building on this ethos, CARA's publishing program amplifies overlooked voices, supporting elder and mid-career practitioners and alternative historiographies. Our books embrace literary and poetic practices; visual, moving-image, and performance art; and radical action as entangled forces shaping how we understand our interconnected worlds. Through the *Invocations* series, CARA furthers its commitment to publishing as a space of resonance – where artistic and intellectual work resists singular narratives. This collaboration with the 36th Bienal de São Paulo strengthens our mission to amplify artists, scholars, and cultural workers whose contributions shape critical discourse, foster new connections, and expand the boundaries of thought.

At CARA, we ask: How can we dream not only about ourselves? This question guides our editorial vision, inviting us to create spaces where knowledge is shared and deepened in dynamic relation. For us, publishing is a process of bringing into generative constellation – where voices converge, entangle, and expand what can be imagined together. This collaboration embodies that ethos, offering books that challenge, unsettle, and inspire new ways of thinking and being in the world.

Manuela Moscoso
Executive and Artistic Director – CARA

The A&L Berg Foundation, founded in 2023 by Allison and Larry Berg, provides access, tools and resources to create, evolve and sustain diverse perspectives and narratives in the United States visual arts. We support and empower individuals committed to making systemic and scalable impact in their practices and communities.

The Foundation's core program is the ESAP Fellowship, which supports and empowers early stage visual arts curators, educators and administrators working in United States arts spaces and institutions. Through building a long-lasting peer support system, and providing navigational tools and opportunities to create expanded professional networks and communities, the Foundation creates equitable visual arts career pathways and ultimately aims to strengthen and diversify the internal ecosystems of United States art institutions.

Our programs provide access to networks, professional development workshops, international research travel, mentorship, relational and soft skills coaching, and financial support for navigating systemic inequities. Each year, a different jury of esteemed arts professionals nominates candidates based on an agreed upon set of criteria, and we invite six of those individuals to participate in the fellowship cohort. Our guest program director, an arts professional who has already successfully navigated the challenges facing the respective cohort, designs the annual program details with a focus on the relational skills that specific cohort requires for career growth.

During the ten-month fellowship, the Foundation provides five empowerment prongs: mentorship with a more established arts professional; relational skills workshops with specialists spanning a variety of industries; an unrestricted financial grant; a robust international research trip opening doors and offering engagement with visual art leaders and peers from every part of the global art ecosystem and ongoing support for professional growth.

A&L Berg Foundation

The Fundação Bienal de São Paulo thanks its partners CARA and A&L Berg Foundation for their special collaboration on the educational publications of the 36th Bienal.

The Federal Government, through the Ministry of Culture, is celebrating the 36th Bienal de São Paulo in partnership with the Fundação Bienal de São Paulo. Just like the great film festivals, the Bienal de São Paulo – the second oldest art biennial in the world – raises enormous expectations on the global exhibition circuit. This year, with the title *Not All Travellers Walk Roads – Of Humanity as Practice,* inspired by a poem by the renowned Brazilian writer Conceição Evaristo, the Bienal reaffirms its vocation as a major showcase for the most current production on the national and global art scene, without losing sight of its wide-ranging educational activities in the formation of new and well-known audiences.

The Ministry of Culture has been working to strengthen the cultural sector through various initiatives and promotion tools. Policies such as the Paulo Gustavo Law and the Aldir Blanc National Policy for the Promotion of Culture encourage other artistic languages, creating opportunities for artists, cultural producers, managers, and visitors. Creating solid conditions for culture means strengthening the creative economy and encouraging the implementation of perennial, permanent, and democratic cultural policies.

Being alongside projects like the Bienal's new movie theater is a source of pride, as it brings together two issues dear to the government: expanding democratic access to cultural facilities combined with an educational arm capable of mediating and making sense of what is on display. By providing free film screenings accompanied by educational activities, another stage is created to strengthen the culture of our country's award-winning and increasingly active audiovisual field.

The Federal Government remains committed to arts and education, which are indispensable fronts for ensuring the right to citizenship and a fairer future for all. We will continue to invest in initiatives that encourage cultural creation and innovation, ensuring that events such as the Bienal de São Paulo continue to inspire and transform generations.

Margareth Menezes
Minister of Culture – Federal Government of Brazil

For more than 35 years, Itaú Cultural (IC) has played a fundamental role in boosting the appreciation of art, culture and education in a complex and heterogeneous society like Brazil. This role is expanded through essential partners for the development of the cultural and creative economy, such as the Fundação Bienal de São Paulo.

Itaú Unibanco is proud to be a sponsor of the Fundação Bienal de São Paulo – it has been for the past 27 years, with this being the 12th edition held in that period – reaffirming its commitment to promoting the visual arts and their transformative role. The Bienal de São Paulo is an important meeting and exchange space for artists, curators, critics, and the public.

In this field, Itaú Cultural organizes actions for enjoyment, education and promotion, including solo and group exhibitions that take place both at its headquarters on Avenida Paulista, 149 (with free admission) and at venues in Brazil's five regions. Highlights of the 2025 exhibitions include *Carlos Zilio – A querela do Brasil*, curated by Paulo Miyada, which will present a retrospective of this artist who, with erudition and irreverence, explored the tensions of Brazilian art. Exhibitions will also be dedicated to the visual artist Rivane Neuenschwander and the curator and critic Paulo Herkenhoff.

Visit itaucultural.org.br to browse the *Filmes e vídeos de artistas* virtual exhibitions, with experimental audiovisual works, and *Livros de artista na Coleção Itaú Cultural*, whose immersive and interactive features allow for detailed appreciation. At Enciclopédia Itaú Cultural (enciclopedia. itaucultural.org.br) you can access hundreds of entries on figures, works, and events in the visual arts.

Being present at the Bienal de São Paulo reinforces our goal of building links with different audiences, valuing the diversity of formats, thoughts, and subjectivities, and fostering creative and critical thinking through Brazilian art and culture.

Itaú Cultural

Bloomberg is proud to sponsor of the 36th edition of the Bienal de São Paulo. For more than a decade we have supported the Bienal's exceptional contemporary art exhibitions in the stunning Ciccillo Matarazzo Pavilion in Ibirapuera Park and around Brazil, through our partnership with Fundação Bienal. This year's edition continues the tradition of presenting captivating and thought-provoking art installations that are free and open to the public.

Every day, Bloomberg connects influential decision makers to a dynamic network of information, people, and ideas. With more than 19,000 employees in 176 offices, Bloomberg delivers business and financial information, news and insight around the world. Our dedication to innovation and new ideas extends to our longstanding support of arts, which we believe are a valuable way to engage citizens and strengthen communities. Through our funding, we help increase access to culture and empower artists and cultural organizations to reach broader audiences.

Bloomberg

For Bradesco, a Brazilian bank *par excellence* that has just celebrated its 83rd anniversary, art and culture are not only fundamental elements in the formation of a people's identity or the construction of their intangible heritage, but also a journey of inclusion and citizenship, a healthy convergence of different points of view. It is, so to speak, a journey towards the new, but with the care to value what is special enough to be history or tradition.

Therefore, when it comes to art and culture, the boundaries between past, present, and future, between form and content, become meaningless. Everything becomes reflection and learning, everything becomes provocation and surprise.

It was on the basis of this interpretation, combined with the positive view of the role of companies in making possible what society considers important, that Bradesco became a sponsor of the 36th edition of the Bienal de São Paulo, undoubtedly one of the most important events in the country aimed at promoting the arts scene, publicizing the various expressions of art and promoting cultural exchange, with all the good that this brings.

By participating in something that is both great and multifaceted, Bradesco shares with the Fundação Bienal de São Paulo – which has organized the event for more than six decades – the goal of democratizing access to culture, multiplying its reach and promoting the appreciation of art.

It's a path with no end, no turning back, full of challenges and at least one certainty: the more people who take part, the better!

Bradesco

Petrobras has a history of more than forty years of continuously believing in culture as a transformational element and a source of energy for society. By supporting unique projects and long-term partnerships, we have built a relationship of respect and collaboration with producers and initiatives all over the country.

The Petrobras Cultural Program has Brazilianness as its guiding element, which is materialized in the themes, origins, curatorship, history, and characteristics of each project we select. By supporting different projects, we put into practice our belief that culture is an important energy that transforms society. We believe that through creativity and inspiration we promote growth and change.

The Bienal de São Paulo is one of the sector's most prestigious events in the country and the world. Petrobras's sponsorship reinforces the company's role in promoting culture in its various forms, consolidating its position as one of the biggest supporters of the arts in Brazil.

Events such as the Bienal de São Paulo make a significant contribution to the economy, promoting innovation, creativity, and sustainability in the economic dynamic. Petrobras is an ally of Brazil's development in its various sectors. It invests in many forms of energy, and culture is certainly one of them.

Petrobras is proud to support Brazilian culture in its plurality of manifestations, taking art to all audiences, all over the country. Because culture is also our energy.

To find out more about the Petrobras Cultural Program, visit petrobras.com.br/cultura.

Petrobras

Instituto Vale Cultural believes in the transformative power of culture. As one of the main supporters of culture in Brazil, it sponsors and promotes projects that foster connections between people, initiatives, and territories. Its commitment is to make culture increasingly accessible and diverse, while also contributing to the strengthening of the creative economy.

It is therefore a pleasure to be part of the realization of this 36th Bienal de São Paulo and its educational program, which explores new formats and approaches. Developed from the *Invocations* proposed by the curatorial team – encounters with poetry, music, performance, and debates that explore notions of humanity across different geographies – the educational program expands the Bienal's communication with diverse audiences and extends its reach beyond the exhibition space and timeframe, in an interdisciplinary way.

With each new edition, the Bienal invites us to rethink art as an exercise in dialogue, in openness to new narratives, and as a space for learning. In this sense, it aligns with the purpose of the Instituto Cultural Vale: to expand opportunities for learning, reflection, new perspectives, and the sharing of art, culture, and education – both inside and outside museums, throughout Brazil.

Where there is culture, Vale is there.

Instituto Cultural Vale

For 110 years, Citi has been part of Brazil's history, accompanying its transformations and driving its development. Our journey is intertwined with that of the country: we are both witnesses to and participants in a Brazil that constantly reinvents itself and moves forward.

More than a financial institution, we believe in the power of culture and education as engines for a more inclusive, innovative, and sustainable future. Investing in these pillars also means celebrating the diversity, creativity, and talent that define the Brazilian spirit.

With this commitment, we are proud, for the first time, to support the 36th Bienal de São Paulo – one of the most important spaces for artistic expression in Latin America, where Brazil thinks, feels, and reinvents itself through art.

We believe in art as an agent of social transformation. Artistic creation has the power to spark dialogue, expand horizons, and inspire new possibilities for the world. By sponsoring the Bienal, we reaffirm our commitment to culture, innovation, and all those who, through art, are building new narratives for both the present and the future.

Citi

Vivo believes in culture as a means of social transformation and is one of the most important brands supporting the visual and performing arts and music in Brazil. Art, like technology, creates connections between people and encourages the search for balance between history, nature and time.

Vivo is currently a sponsor of the most important museums in Brazil, such as the Museu de Arte de São Paulo Assis Chateaubriand (MASP), the Pinacoteca de São Paulo, the Museu da Imagem e do Som (MIS-São Paulo), the Museu Afro Brasil Emanoel Araujo, the Museu de Arte Moderna de São Paulo (MAM SP), as well as the Instituto Inhotim and the Palácio das Artes, both in Minas Gerais, and the Museu Oscar Niemeyer, in Paraná.

Teatro Vivo, located in São Paulo, offers a curated selection of contemporary plays that promote reflection on current issues and value cultural diversity. In addition, it is a fully accessible space, offering resources such as translation into Libras (Brazilian sign language), audio descriptions and trained staff, ensuring inclusion for people with disabilities and reduced mobility. In 2024, it welcomed over 50,000 people.

The brand also supports projects in the world of music that are genuinely Brazilian and regional, reinforcing its proximity with local culture at iconic and traditional events in our country, such as the Parintins Festival, Galo da Madrugada, the Çairé Festival, Lollapalooza, The Town, and Vivo Música.

The brand's initiatives in the cultural sphere broaden access to knowledge with new ways of experiencing and learning, strengthened by the aspects of diversity, sustainability, inclusion and education. All information is gathered and shared on the @vivo.cultura and @vivo Instagram profiles.

Vivo

Confronted with the incessant problems of humanity, perhaps it is worth dwelling a little longer on some open questions, taking sustenance from resources that allow us to dig and build answers procedurally. In this sense, art, in its many guises, offers fertile ground for critical elaborations about the world and ourselves.

The meeting of art and education – both understood as fields of knowledge – enables the torsion of time and space: it becomes possible, thus, to suspend neutralities and dilate what is precipitated in structures. How far is this approach able to infer the real and interfere in it? It allows us to (re)populate imaginaries, to unpick the universalizing statute attributed to concepts, practices and people, and thus to carve out reality with narratives that articulate the individual and the collective, in a procedural and coherent manner regarding the issues that permeate existence.

It is according to this panorama that Sesc São Paulo and the Fundação Bienal, through the 35th Bienal de São Paulo, reiterate their long-standing partnership, a mutual commitment to fostering experiences of coexistence with the visual arts, expanding access to cultural actions and the exercise of otherness.

This partnership, which has been established and renewed for over a decade, has led to the promotion of projects such as simultaneous exhibitions, public meetings, seminars and training for educators, as well as the consolidated itinerant exhibition with excerpts from the Bienal in Sesc units in the wider state of São Paulo. The confluence of choices and propositions is part of the institutional perspective of culture as a right, and conceives, together with one of the largest exhibitions in the country, an accessible horizon for contemporary art in Brazil.

Sesc São Paulo

Foreword
Fundação Bienal de São Paulo

This book is an extension of the investigations into notions of humanity in different parts of the world, engaging with the ideas of the 36th Bienal de São Paulo – *Not All Travellers Walk Roads – Of Humanity as Practice*, from *Invocation #3, Mawali-Taqsim: Improvisation as a Space and Technology of Humanity*, which took place in Zanzibar in February 2025.

The *Invocations* are meetings with presentations of poetry, research, music, and dance that precede the exhibition in São Paulo. In addition to Zanzibar, they also took place in three other territories: Marrakech, Guadeloupe, and Tokyo, between November 2024 and April 2025.

In the lyrics of Luiz Gonzaga's "O bom improvisador" [The good improviser], a poet who can't find his rhyme symbolizes a sad world that is out of order, without beauty or meaning:

> When the good improviser
> Is missing a rhyme
> It's like a heart
> When love is missing[1]

In this song by the "Rei do Baião" [King of Baião], Zé Canário, Andorinha, and Sabiá are the bird-musicians who remind us that rhythm and improvised rhymes infuse both the grand and the everyday with grace and significance. They accompany us here on a journey from Brazil to Zanzibar, the stunning archipelago in the Indian Ocean, home to the *Taarab* musical tradition and the site of *Invocation* #3. This publication gathers documentation of the event, conversations with artists and intellectuals, and educational practices developed by the Bienal team, which converge on a common element: *improvisation.*

From the records of the Zanzibar *Invocation* to the material created to engage with the reality of Brazilian education, improvisation emerges as a compelling metaphor for human adaptability and interconnection. This theme is particularly resonant in the essays exploring the historical and cultural dimensions of Taarab in the context of the *Invocation.*

In "Engaging with the 36th Bienal de São Paulo," Khamis Muhamed Juma underscores the importance of Taarab in Zanzibar, tracing its influence on the archipelago's music, visual arts, and culture. The author identifies the Taarab as a tool for cultural and artistic exchange in which contemporary art and local traditions connect, invoking the past, present, and future. The creative spirit of Taarab shapes the territory and articulates itself with history, memory, and identity, nurturing future generations.

The debate on the current state of Taarab is also present in "History of Taarab in Zanzibar and Worldwide," by Bi Mariam Hamdani, who writes about the musical style's relevance and presence in East Africa and various other parts of the world, addressing groups that have been important in this trajectory. In "My Journey in Taarab Music," singer Rukia Ramadhani shares a personal narrative reflecting on the experiences of women in the Taarab scene, navigating both recognition and prejudice. This kind of experience also appears in the transcript of the speech by Aisha Bakary, the DJ and producer internationally known as Hijab DJ.

In "Taarab: An Audience Experience in the Heart of Zanzibar," Mohamed Ameir Muombwa offers a vivid account of attending a performance in Zanzibar, exploring how sensory, emotional, and intellectual responses – alongside the symbolism of colors on stage – reveal the genre's aesthetic and political dimensions. He also acknowledges the contributions of Tryphon Evarist, who also collaborates in this publication.

Halda Mohamed Alkanaan introduces the Dhow Countries Music Academy, an institution dedicated to preserving the musical heritage of the Indian Ocean coast and the Arabian Gulf. The school focuses on improvisation and the creative adaptation of traditional art forms

24

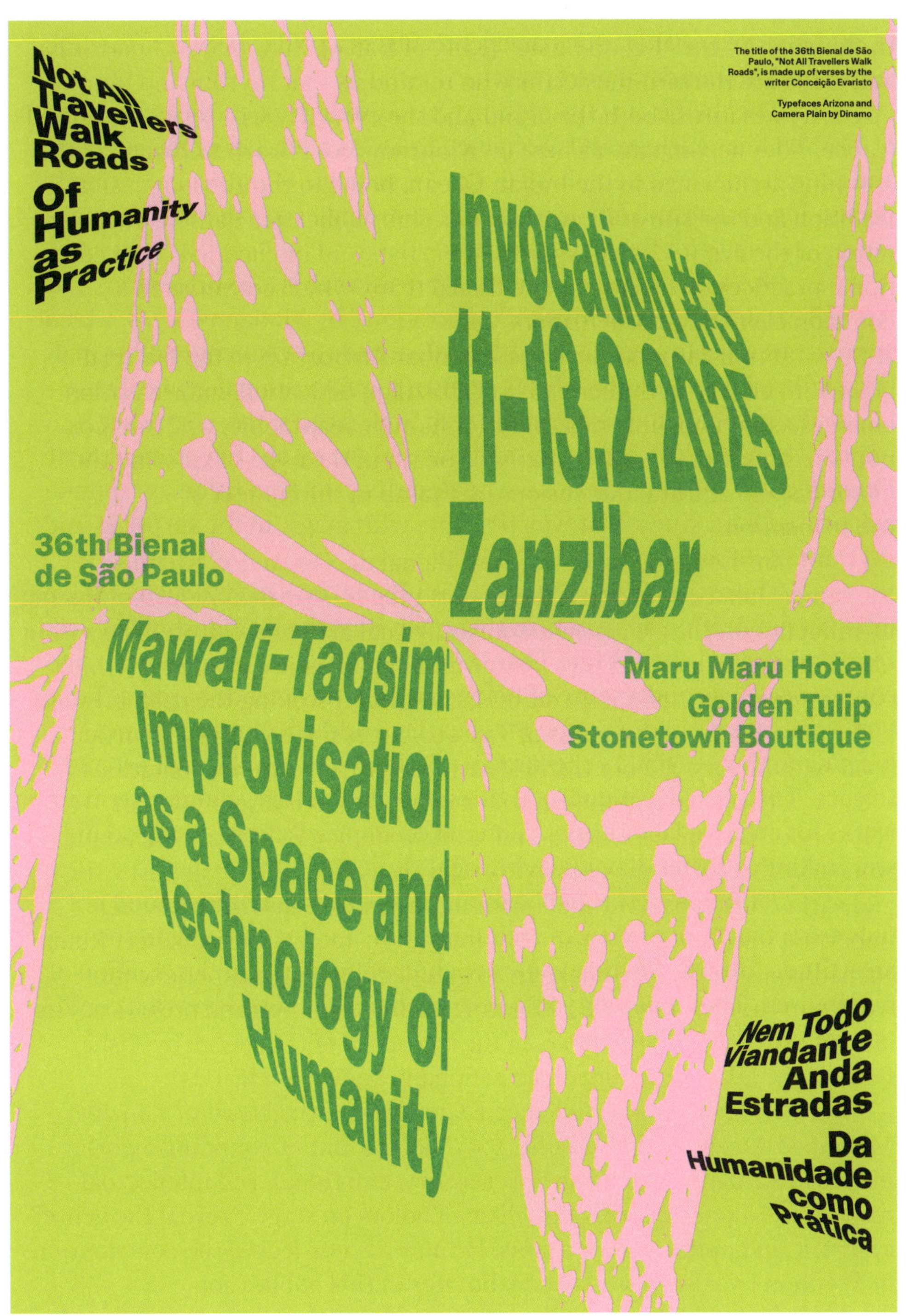

Poster of the *Invocation* #3, 11-13 February, 2025
© Studio Yukiko / Fundação Bienal de São Paulo

in response to global artistic trends, serving as a bridge between Taarab's legacy and contemporary art practices.

The theme of transmission runs as well through the contributions of Thabit Omar Kiringe and Mohamed Ilyas. As a teacher of music theory and composer, Kiringe emphasizes the importance of musical notation for preserving Taarab and advocates for new strategies to safeguard Zanzibar's musical heritage for future generations.

The idea of music as a form of resistance is also present in "The Art of Taarab Poetry and Music Composition," by Mohamed Ilyas, which approaches ways to keep the tradition alive and the challenges of formalizing it through notation as this is such an improvisational genre. These ideias also resonate in the poem "Taarab," by sound artist, composer, and improviser Ajíteñà Marco Scarassatti, and in the essay "Experiment, with *Fundamento*," by Allan da Rosa, who describes improvisation as "spontaneity fused with study, that which adapts with magic to the surprises and rhythms of its surroundings."

The artists featured in the 36th Bienal de São Paulo who took part into this publication approach, in their own way, the relationship between sound and knowledge. While Thania Petersen explores how rhythm can convey resilience and a sense of belonging that transcends borders, Tanka Fonta celebrates children's openness to the world of color and sound, locating in this sensibility the human potential to learn through art and science. The two educational activities included in this volume offer frameworks for creative laboratories centered on improvisation – using sound and storytelling to foster dialogue with local contexts.

Throughout this publication, improvisation is understood not only from the point of view of technique, but as a way of being in the world, an attitude towards life that values openness, fluidity, and the creation of possibilities. Thus, humanity as a verb becomes the revelation of a condition: improvising is human.

1   Luiz Gonzaga, "O bom improvisador" [The good improviser], composition: Luiz Gonzaga and Nelson Valença, album: *Luiz Gonzaga*, 1973.

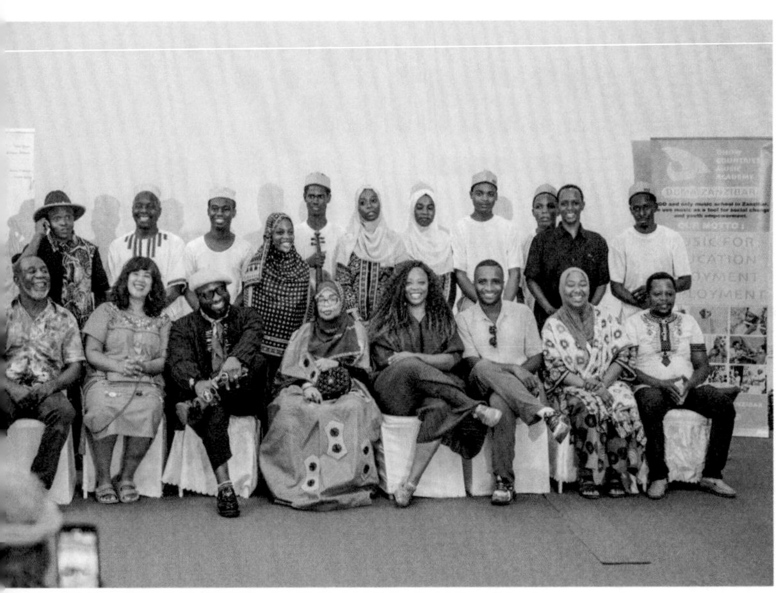

All photos, unless otherwise stated: © Aden Rajab Said / Fundação Bienal de São Paulo

The Humanity of Taarab

Bonaventure Soh Bejeng Ndikung

Asalam Aleykum!
Habari za jioni na karibu kwenye tukio
hili la Bienal de São Paulo.
Tunamshukuru uwepo wenu nasi.[1]

Good evening and welcome to the *Invocation* #3 of the 36th Bienal de São Paulo.

After engaging with varying notions of humanity and with the different shades and inflections of humanity in Marrakech, and the Mediterranean Sea, and Guadeloupe at the Atlantic Ocean, we are both humbled and profoundly grateful to be with you now in Zanzibar, surrounded by the Swahili Sea, also known as the Indian Ocean.

I'd like to begin by thanking the Fundação Bienal de São Paulo and all my colleagues in São Paulo and beyond, especially the conceptual team: Keyna, Thiago, Anna, Alya, and Henriette, the Dhow Countries Music Academy (particularly Halda Mohamed Alkanaan, Khamis Juma, Tryphon Evarist, and chairperson Salma Adim), our producer Thureiya Saeed Saleh, our co-conspirator Ben Ntahondi, our hosts Maru Maru and Golden Tulip, and our supporters YAS (above all, Hassanein Hiridjee and Margaux Huille).

Before proceeding, allow me to ground this moment with a poem, titled "Only Voice Remains," by the Persian poet Forugh Farrokhzad:

Why should I stop, why?
Birds have gone to seek their blue way.
The horizon is horizontal,
movement vertical – a gushing geyser.
Bright stars spin as far as the eye can see.
The Earth repeats itself in space, air tunnels
become connecting canals and day changes
to an entity so vast it cannot be stuffed
into the narrow imaginations of the newspaper worms.
Why should I stop?
The path meanders among life's tiny veins
and the climate of the moon's womb will annihilate
the cancerous cells, and in the chemical aura of after-dawn
there will remain only voice –
                    voice seeping into time.
Why should I stop?
What is a swamp but a spawning ground
for corruption's vermin?
Swelled corpses pen the morgue's thoughts,
the cad hides his yellowness in the dark,
and the cockroach
… ah when the cockroach harangues,
                    why should I stop?
Printer's lead letters line up in vain.
Lead letters in league cannot salvage petty thoughts.
My essence is of trees; breathing stale air depresses me.
A bird long dead counseled me to remember flight.
Fusion creates the greatest force –
fusion with the sun's luminescent soul,
comprehension flooding with light.
Windmills eventually warp and rot.
Why should I stop?
I hold to my breasts sheaves of unripe wheat
and give them milk.
Voice, voice, only voice.
The water's voice, its wish to flow,
the starlight's voice pouring upon the earth's female form,
the voice of the egg in the womb congealing into sense,
the clotting together of love's minds.
Voice, voice, voice, only voice remains.
In a world of runts,

measurements orbit around zero.
Why must I stop?
The four elements alone rule me;
my heart's charter cannot be drafted
by the provincial government of the blind.
What have I to do with the long feral howls
of the beasts' genitals?
What have I to do with the slow progress
of a maggot through flesh?
It's the flowers' bloodstained history that has committed me to life,
the flowers' bloodstained history, you hear?[2]

There are various translations of this seminal poem, some titled "Only Voice Remains," others "Only Sound Remains." But when Farrokhzad writes of voice, she is not merely referring to the human voice. Rather, she invokes the voices of the sea and wind, of plants and stones, of maggots and corals, of birds and all beings – animate or not (if such a distinctions can even be made).

On my way to Zanzibar this morning, a dear artist friend reminded me of this poem, and since then, one line has echoed in my mind over and over again: "there will remain only voice – voice seeping into time."

It prompted me to think of our voices as humanity's finger print and of our voices as the mediators between us and the worlds we inhabit or wish to inhabit. Our voices as the spaces of evidence, of revelations, as traces of our struggles and delights, our losses and longings. It is through our voices that we shape, articulate, and sculpt our humanities. And it is by listening to the voices of other beings that we truly come into relation.

"There will remain only voice – voice seeping into time."

For this *Invocation*, we have chosen to focus on the voice of Taarab – not only as a musical genre, but as a technology, a philosophy, a way of being in the world. The voice of Taarab seeps into time and is steeped in poetry. The songs of great Taarab musicians like Siti bint Saad, Bi Kidude, Mzee Yusuph and many others speak of personal and social issues, of love and politics, of the brighter and darker sides of life and humanity. Like great poetry, good Taarab has the potential of opening sacred worlds.

The title of this edition of the Bienal de São Paulo – *Not All Travelers Walk Roads* – comes from a poem by Afro-Brazilian writer Conceição Evaristo: "Da calma e do silêncio" [Of Calm and Silence].[3] It's very interesting to follow the lines that come before and after what became the title: "When my feet slow down, please, don't force me. Walk for what? Let me fall, leave me alone, in apparent inertia. Not all

31

travelers walk roads, there are submerged worlds, that only the silence of poetry penetrates." And the same applies to Taarab: there are submerged worlds that only its rhythms, idioms, and stories can reach.

"There will remain only voice – voice seeping into time."

This takes me to the voice of Khamis Abeid in his 1964 hit "Dunia Rangi Mbili" [Two-Faced World], originally written by master poet Haji Gora Haji in 1959. In Abeid's performance, Gora Haji's words, in Abeid's mouth, become the voice of the people. Here, Taarab music serves as both vessel and catalyst – carrying philosophical reflections, political commentary, emotional truths, and and lyrical notes. Haji Gora Haji wrote:

This two-faced world
Goodness comes first
The world is unpredictable

Lick the honey
People make you feel happy
Your [life] is fulfilled
I remember well
And then there's wickedness
It can turn against you

Raise your dignity
Whatever you say is always right
By whatever you intend to do.[4]

This song was composed just one year after Zanzibar became fully independent from Britain in 1963, and in the year of the Zanzibar Revolution (Mapinduzi ya Zanzibar), 1964. Thus, it arose at a time of uncertain transitions, self-determination, drawing lessons from the past and planning for the future.

There are many ways to interpret the two-faced world of Haji Gora Haji's poem. Obviously, one might think in terms of oppositions – good/bad, beauty/ugliness, joy/pain, love/hate – and it would be a valid, albeit rushed, reading of the poem. But what if we imagined theses faces not as opposites but as pluralities? As a multiplicity that, when combined, becomes greater than the sum of its parts? What if this notion of two faces became a multitude of faces? Zanzibar is indeed a multi-faced world. As a whole, it is greater than the sum of its parts, which are largely African. Its cultural richness stems from Bantu, Shirazi, Arab, and Indian influences, among others. This multi-faced-worldliness manifests in the Swahili language – a convergence of various Bantu languages with borrowed elements from Arabic, Portuguese, German, English, Hindustani, Persian, Malay, and others. It is also noteworthy the fact that this plurality manifests in the music genre Taarab, that is basically the culmination of multiple worlds and expressions, a multiplicity of expressions of humanity, with African, Arabic, European, and Asian roots.

As Hilda Kiel points out in her essay "Travel on a Song – The Roots of Zanzibar Taarab,"[5] the etymology of the word Taarab, in Arabic, "means 'to be moved (with joy or grief)', 'to be delighted or enraptured as well as 'to make music', 'to sing, vocalize or chant',"[6] and Taarab expresses "a state of being, an elevated, if not ecstatic state of mind that is induced by the pleasure of listening to music."

We came to Zanzibar, with this *Invocation* for the Bienal de São Paulo, precisely because of Taarab's ability to so eloquently express and embody our joys and grieves, delightedness and enrapturing, to so felicitously capture this ecstatic state of being, while articulating, at the same time, the cultures of the people of the Swahili Sea – that crossroad, that junction of cultures, uniting peoples, histories of trades, intermarriages, explorations and exploitations, a space of encounters of civilizations, the manifestation of geopolitics and geopoetics, as well as the two-faced world of greatness and meanness of humankind...

"There will remain only voice – voice seeping into time."

While we are interested in Taarab at large for this *Invocation* #3, our particular focus lies in the spaces and notions of improvisation within Taarab.

In the interview "How Improvisation Saved My Life,"[7] the South African master composer and pianist Abdullah Ibrahim recounts an anecdote from an Apartheid-era Cape Town. He describes how, after being arrested by the police, he might have been executed had he not improvised. "When you see that gang (police) coming around the corner toward you," he said, "you better improvise." And he did – by rushing into a police station and spinning a story about turtle doves, cooing as he spoke.

Improvisation in music is the space where one permits oneself to go off script, to express deeper intentions than those formally assigned or written, to manifest sentiments, political perspectives, and emotional truths that transcend the annotated or formally composed. It is, in both literal and metaphorical terms, a space of "otherwise" communication with the listener. One might say that the space of improvisation is where humanity is conjugated.

As Kiel points out in her aforementioned essay, Mawali expresses, in Swahili Taarab, vocal improvisations, while Taqsim or Taqasim denotes instrumental improvisation(s).

33

In their article "We Make up the Rules as We Go Along: Improvisation as an Essential Aspect of Human Practices?", Alessandro Bertinetto and Georg W. Bertram argue that "human reason lies in the concept of improvisation. Making up the rules as one goes along is, by definition, an improvisatory practice." They claim that "human beings establish normative practices by improvising within the situations they are living through, a phenomenon well exemplified by artistic improvisation," and they propose that "important dimensions of human practices (normativity, habit, and freedom) can only be adequately understood by taking into account their constitutive connection to improvisation."[8]

"There will remain only voice – voice seeping into time."

In the days to come, a wide range of contributors will help us unfold the poetics and politics of Taarab, with particular attention to Mawali and Taqsim as technologies for expressing the many faces of our worlds and humanities. We will allow ourselves to be guided by Haji Gora Haji's reflections on the unpredictability of the world.

These *Invocations* held across the globe should be understood as efforts of feeling the pulse of humanity – across different time zones, geographies, climates, and social pressures – before staging the Bienal in São Paulo. They allow us to listen to the full spectrum of humanity's voices, accents, shapes, tastes, and forms. Through them, we bring the Bienal de São Paulo to the world, and, in turn, we bring the world to São Paulo.

As Forugh Farrokhzad's poem "Only Voice Remains" questions: Why should we stop, why? We must continue to listen – to the voice of the stars and to that of the water, of the egg, of the mangrove, and to our own voices, to each other. And we will continue to lend our voices to mark and shape spaces, and places, and most especially the future – toward a more expansive vision of what it means to be human. As Farrokhzad says "Fusion creates the greatest force – fusion with the sun's luminescent soul, comprehension flooding with light." Taarab is that fusion – of human voices, the voices of instruments and of the sea, with the sun's luminescent soul.

And when we are all gone:
"There will remain only voice – voice seeping into time."

Thank you very much.

1   Peace be upon you! Good evening and welcome to this event of the Bienal de São Paulo.

2   Forugh Farrokhzad, *Sin: Selected Poems of Forugh Farrokhzad*. Translated by Sholeh Wolpé. Fayetteville: University of Arkansas Press, 2008.

3   Conceição Evaristo, "Da calma e do silêncio". In: *Poemas da recordação e outros movimentos.* Belo Horizonte: Nandyala, 2008.

4   "Dunia Rangi Mbili," written by Haji Gora Haji and sung by Khamis Abeid.

5   Hilda Kiel, "Travel on a Song – The Roots of Zanzibar Taarab." *African Music: Journal of International Library of African Music*, v. 9, no. 2, 2012.

6   Hans Wehr, *Dictionary of Modern Written Arabic*. Wiesbaden: Otto Harrassowitz, 1976.

7   Available at www.youtube.com/watch?v=Cx-PbqtQMtk. Accessed in Mar. 2025.

8   Alessandro Bertinetto and Georg W. Bertram, "We Make Up the Rules as We Go Along: Improvisation as an Essential Aspect of Human Practices?". *Open Philosophy*, v. 3, 2020, pp. 202–221.

Engaging with the 36th Bienal de São Paulo

Khamis Muhamed Juma

As the director of the Dhow Countries Music Academy (DCMA), it is with deep respect and admiration that I present an exploration of the 36th Bienal de São Paulo's *Invocation #3, Mawali-Taqsim: Improvisation as a Space and Technology of Humanity*, held in the historic and culturally rich island of Zanzibar – a place where diverse histories converge through music, art, and community.

In this publication, we delve into the intimate relationship between contemporary art and the living traditions that have shaped Zanzibar, particularly Taarab music, which has served as the heartbeat of the island's cultural expression for over a century.

The theme of this Bienal, *Not All Travellers Walk Roads – Of Humanity as Practice*, aptly echoes Zanzibar's profound role as a site of cultural and artistic exchange, where global narratives intertwine with local histories. The art presented in the Bienal summoned the voices of the past, the struggles of the present, and the possibilities of a collective future. Yet, within this broader framework of global art, it is essential to reflect on the rich, indigenous musical heritage of Zanzibar, where Taarab has long been a medium through which its people have expressed joy, sorrow, and hope.

Taarab music, with its intricate rhythms, poetic lyrics, and cross-cultural influences, has been a vital force in Zanzibar's cultural life for generations. When we reflect on the idea of *Invocation*, it becomes evident that Taarab itself, much like art in general, is a form of invocation – an ongoing process that calls upon memory, identity, and history. Deeply rooted in the island's Arab, Swahili, and African heritage, Taarab's evolution mirrors the complexities of Zanzibar's cultural and political transformations.

Throughout this volume, we engage with key figures who have shaped the Taarab tradition and ensured its ongoing relevance, such as the legendary Siti bint Saad, celebrated singer Mariam Hamdani, composers and performers Mohamed Ilyas, Rukia Ramadhani, Siti Muharam, Tryphon Evarist, and many others whose voices and presence continue to inspire both local and global Taarab communities. Their contributions to this genre cannot be overstated; they are more than performers – they are curators of Zanzibar's rich cultural memory and stewards of its evolving artistic future.

We must also acknowledge Mr. Thabit Omar Kiringe, a Swahili music composer and educator whose work in transcribing Taarab lyrics has been vital to preserving the poetic dimension of this tradition, allowing for it to resonate with both contemporary and future audiences. As a teacher, Mr. Thabit has mentored generations of musicians and lyricists, ensuring that the art of Swahili songwriting is passed down with integrity and imbued with timeless relevance and meaning.

37 The conversations around *Invocation #3* of the 36th Bienal de São

Paulo cannot be fully accomplished without acknowledging the significance of Taarab music for Zanzibar's cultural identity. For years, Taarab music has served as a powerful vehicle for invoking the past, honoring the ancestral connections between Zanzibar and its diverse communities, while also pushing the boundaries of cultural expression, opening up new realms of innovation.

The symbiotic relationship between Taarab and contemporary visual art is significant. Like other art forms, Taarab is ever-evolving, incorporating influences from both traditional sounds and global genres. It resonates deeply with the Bienal's themes, which question the historical and contemporary influences that shape the world. Just as the artists in the Bienal grapple with tensions between past and present, so does Taarab – a genre that has long navigated the complexity of colonial legacies, cultural adaptation, and the aspiration to preserve Zanzibar's singular identity amidst global influences.

This event serves not only as a record of the *Invocation #3* in Zanzibar, but also as a testament to the living art form of Taarab music – a powerful, evocative tradition that continues to shape the island's cultural and artistic landscape. The intertwining of these two worlds – contemporary visual art and the enduring legacy of Taarab – reminds us of the power of invocation itself. Whether through the spoken word of an artist's exhibition or the lyrical cadence of a Taarab song, both mediums call on us to reflect, to remember, and to respond.

In the words that follow, we hear not only the voices of the artists featured in the Bienal, but also the voices of those who have been immersed in the world of Taarab for decades. Their stories, contributions, and reflections on the intersection of music, art, and culture remind us of the importance of engaging with our legacies, nurturing the future generations of creators, and invoking the power of art to heal, connect, and transform.

Through the powerful legacies of figures like Mohamed Ilyas, Mariam Hamdani, and Mr. Thabit, alongside the participating artists of the Bienal, we understand the enduring relevance of the past as we lay the foundation for the future. Their contibutions in music, education, and visual arts invite us to consider not only what we have inherited, but also how we might continue to invoke, adapt, and transmit the creative spirit that defines Zanzibar.

In closing, these words stand as a celebration of culture and memory, and a call to action: for all who engage with this work to reflect, participate, and chart new paths forward. Through the intersection of art and music, we uncover the many layers of Zanzibar's cultural fabric – ensuring that its voices, both past and present, are not silenced, but continue to be heard throughout the world.

My Journey in Taarab Music

Rukia Ramadhani

It is a great honor to stand before you today and share the story of my life's journey in Taarab music – a tradition deeply rooted in the cultural identity of Zanzibar and the Swahili Coast. Music has been my voice, my passion, and my way of contributing to the preservation of our rich heritage.

I was born on December 29, 1958, in Wete, Pemba, but at the age of two I moved with my mother to Unguja, Zanzibar, where I grew up in Mwembe Shauri Town. From an early age, I was immersed in music and performance, which became an essential part of my life.

I first discovered my love for singing at Raha Leo Nursery School, and later at Kidutani Primary School, where I began performing at national celebrations such as the commemoration of Free Education in Zanzibar. My music teachers, Khamis Shekhe and Said Mwinyi, played an important role in shaping my early musical skills.

While attending Kidutani Secondary School, I continued to perform at celebratory events and in Qaseeda (Islamic devotional music). It was also during this time that I was introduced to the Culture Musical Club, one of Zanzibar's most renowed Taarab institutions. This marked the beginning of my professional career as a Taarab artist.

At the same time, I joined the Mwembe Shauri Branch Music Group, where I developed my performance skills and gained recognition as a singer. After completing my education, I worked in a few government offices, including the Ministry of Information, the Ministry of Constitution and Governance, and finally, the Ministry of Constitution and Laws, serving as a secretary.

However, my passion for music never faded. I officially left the Mwembe Shauri Branch Music Group and dedicated myself fully to the Culture Musical Club, where I had the opportunity to perform internationally in countries such as France, Germany, Luxembourg, Austria, and Spain.

Later in my career, I joined Nadi Ikhwan Safaa, Zanzibar's oldest Taarab orchestra, where my reputation as a musician and performer grew even further. This prestigious group allowed me to showcase my talent on the global stage, performing in Spain, Belgium, and Finland, sharing the rich traditions of Zanzibari Taarab with audiences around the world.

Challenges as a Female Taarab Artist in Zanzibar

Being a woman in the Taarab music scene has never been easy, especially in a predominantly Islamic society like Zanzibar, where female performers have historically faced public scrutiny and harsh criticism.

When I began performing, many viewed women in the music scene as rebellious, immoral, or unsuitable for public life. I was often called names like "Muhuni" (a derogatory term implying a wayward or undisciplined person) simply for following my passion for music. This was because women in music were seen as challenging traditional gender roles, and performing in front of men was considered improper.

Despite these challenges, I refused to be discouraged. I remained committed to my art, which was fostered by my dedication, professionalism, and talent, proving that a woman can be both a musician and a respected member of society. Over time, as more women entered the Taarab scene, public perception began to shift – but the struggle for acceptance and recognition persists.

Challenges Female Artists Face Today

Even in today's world, female musicians still face discrimination and challenges in the industry. Some of these include: lack of respect from male counterparts – many female artists struggle to be recognized and respected in their field, as some male musicians refuse to acknowledge the contributions of women; egos in the industry – many younger artists today fail to acknowledge and honor their teachers and mentors, overlooking the dedication and sacrifices that ensured the preservation of Taarab music; limited opportunities and funding – women often receive fewer opportunities to record, perform, or travel compared to their male counterparts; cultural expectations – some still believe that a woman's place is at home, and choosing a career in music is seen as improper.

Despite these obstacles, women continue to persevere, breaking stereotypes and carving out their rightful place in the music industry.

My Contributions and Achievements in Taarab

In addition to singing, I have explored musical instrumentation, learning to play the *ngoma* (bongo drums), and I am currently studying the keyboard to further expand my musical skills.

My contributions to Taarab have been recognized with several awards and distinctions both in Zanzibar and Dar es Salaam. While many of these honors were for my Taarab performances, one was specifically awarded for Qaseeda, underscoring my versatility as a musician.

Preserving Taarab for Future Generations

As Taarab continues to evolve, it is vital to preserve its original form while embracing modern influences. Music notation, archiving, and mentorship are crucial to ensure that future generations inherit the richness of this genre.

Throughout my career, I have sought to inspire young artists and encourage them to embrace both the traditional and innovative elements of Taarab. Music education plays a key role in transmitting the oral traditions, intricate melodies, and the poetic depth of this unique art form.

Taarab is more than music – it is a way of life, a repository of history, and a living legacy. It carries our stories, emotions, and cultural heritage, keeping our traditions alive. I am deeply grateful for the opportunity to share my journey with you all at the 36th Bienal de São Paulo, *Invocation #3*, and to celebrate the power of music, poetry, and improvisation in shaping our world.

As we continue to explore and celebrate Zanzibari Taarab, let us remember that music is a bridge between past, present, and future, connecting people across generations and cultures.

Uwaridi Female Band

Uwaridi Female Band is a dynamic all-women ensemble composed of passionate and skilled musicians. The group showcases a rich variety of instruments, including the violin, accordion, tabla, cajon, *ngoma, zeze,* rimba, *sanduku, kidumbaki, rika,* and various other percussion instruments.

The band preserves Zanzibar's cultural heritage while propelling it forward by fusing traditional sounds with modern arrangements. The members compose their own original pieces, drawing inspiration from a diverse repertoire that includes traditional Taarab, Ngoma, Gogo music, Kidumbak, and other exciting fusions.

Comprised of ten members – alumni of the Dhow Countries Music Academy and seasoned music educators –, the band has performed on both international stages and at local venues.

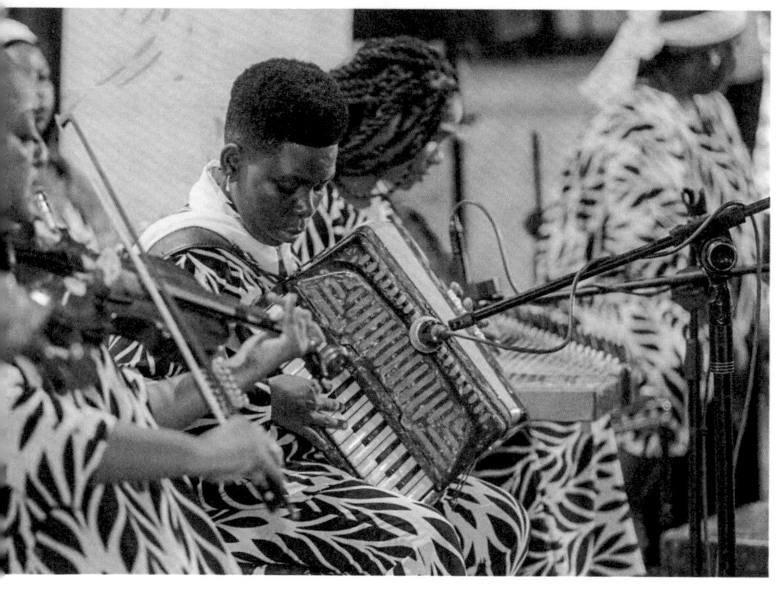

Performance
documentation

Siti Muharam

One of the most prominent contemporary singers from Zanzibar, Siti Muharam has transformed what was once formal court music into a more intimate and improvisational form – infused with a spirit of inclusivity that combined Arabic and Swahili lyrics. In doing so, she paved the way for other female Taarab singers, including Bi Kidude.

Today, Siti Muharam carries forward the life and legacy of her legendary great grandmother, Siti Binti Saad. With support from The Vinyl Factory, Songlines, Pan African Music, British radio DJs Gilles Peterson and Tom Ravenscroft and enthusiastic praise from *The Guardian*, *The Financial Times*, *The Wire* and *Mojo*, her debut release, *Siti of Unguja*, is poised to be recognized as one of the top African music albums of 2020.

Performance documentation

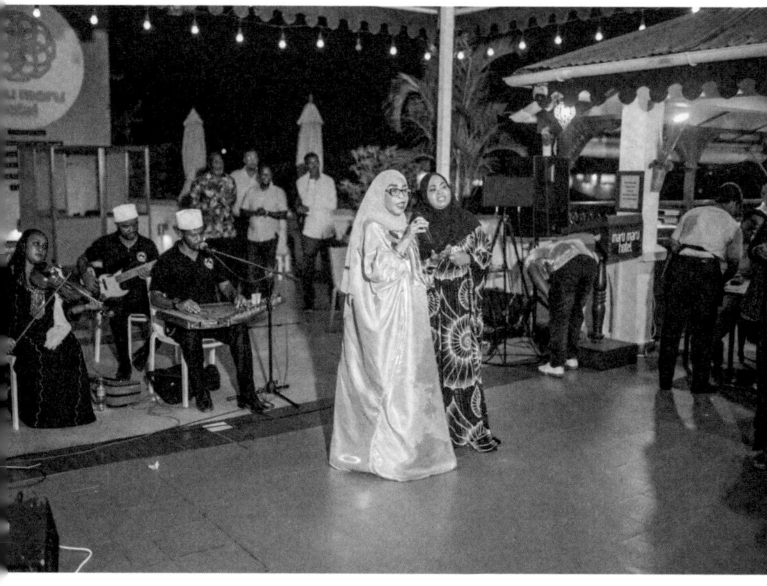

Music as a Repository of Transoceanic Memory

conversation with Thania Petersen

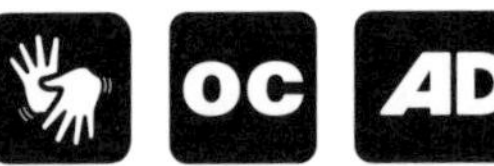

Text developed from a
conversation between the
Fundação Bienal team, Anna Roberta
Goetz (co-curator of the 36th Bienal),
and the artist in March, 2025.

Bienal de São Paulo Team: Your artistic practice often explores the complexities of identity and history, especially in the context of South Africa. How do your personal experiences as a descendant of Tuan Guru[1] and as a Muslim woman from Cape Town shape your artistic work and the stories you choose to tell?

Thania Petersen: Since its arrival in the Cape, Islam has always stood as a force of resistance against colonialism and apartheid. For centuries, people have turned to Islam and the Muslim community as one of the few sources of opposition to the oppressive systems imposed upon us. Through our rituals, transcendental practices, and music, enslaved and oppressed communities found an escape from their harsh realities. Islam offered liberation through divine love and created spaces for communities to thrive based on compassion rather than violence.

This ideology formed the foundation of our community and our liberation struggle, and became so powerful that it was eventually banned. It's deeply unsettling to witness the misrepresentation and misunderstanding of this faith, which has always served as a source of liberation for us. The rise of Islamophobia globally baffles me, and I feel a responsibility to inform others about the true, liberating role Islam has played in our histories.

As a child of Cape Town, I was inevitably born into a lineage of fighters. My community, shaped by the enduring legacies of colonialism, displacement, and apartheid, carries the burden of a long history of resistance. This city – its streets, its stories – echoes the voices of those who fought, resisted, and survived. We are descendants of those who faced systemic oppression and yet remained resilient, creating spaces of survival and defiance in the face of adversity.

For me, the memory of Tuan Guru is central to this lineage. He is not just a historical figure to be admired; he is a connection to our past, an anchor that ties us to the Indian Ocean and to ancestral lands far beyond Cape Town. Tuan Guru's story is one of strength and knowledge – his arrival in the Cape as a prisoner of war, his eventual freedom, and his role in establishing Islam in this land. He embodies the spirit of resilience and cultural perseverance. His story connects us to the wider world and the rich traditions and wisdom brought to our shores through Indian Ocean trade routes. His memory serves as a bridge between the struggles of the past and the possibilities of the future, and is a reminder that we have been shaped not only by the violence of colonization but also by a rich heritage of practices, knowledge, and faith that span oceans and generations.

As his descendant, I carry that connection deeply. My work and

49

creative expression are rooted in the ritual practices that have been handed down through generatios, continuing that heritage.

    Anna Roberta Goetz: Your multidisciplinary artistic practice over the last decade has been guided by looking at how different communities around the globe are connected through their everyday practices. Despite being separated by colonization and forced to migration and marginalization, they share a cultural heritage. And so you trace and analyze shared traditions and thus render new cultural geographies of communality and solidarity. In what way are you expanding on this approach in your new work for the Bienal de São Paulo? What were the initial questions that guided your research?

TP: I find it incredibly fascinating how displaced communities with shared ancestries often develop remarkably similar cultural practices and traditions – especially in music – even when isolated from one another. For the Bienal de São Paulo, I chose to further explore music as a repository of transoceanic memory. After studying Creole music from the Cape and Suriname, for instance, I realized these communities are linked not only by the all too often mentioned violent history of forced migration and colonialism, but also by shared African, Indonesian and possibly Indigenous genetic ancestry that is reflected in their music.

    In the music of my own community, I see how rhythm, tone, and texture express resilience, survival, and a profound sense of belonging that transcends boundaries. The polyrhythms, syncopation, call-and-response patterns, and melodies passed down in Cape Town are identical to those in Suriname. They speak of embodied experience, collective memory. There's power in how sound serves both as a reflection of past struggles and as a symbol of triumph.

    Despite their geographic isolation, these communities developed a near-identical musical language. For centuries, our communities have creolized, blending different heritages, but the music has remained remarkably consistent. How is it possible? How did the *Kaapse Klopse* of Cape Town and the Creole music of Suriname, which evolved separately, end up with such strikingly similar musical textures? This question haunted me. It made me reflect on the idea that sound and rhythm might be something inherited, something encoded in our DNA. Perhaps they serve a spiritual function, reconnecting us across time and space. Perhaps our emotional, psychological, and historical experiences live on in the rhythms we carry within our bodies – our ancestors' voices and sounds manifesting

50

through music. This reflection led me to consider the idea of sonic genetics: the possibility that a community's experiences – its history, migration, trauma, joy, and resilience – are not only passed down through stories, rituals, and practices, but also bodily encoded in its people's very DNA.

Traditionally, we think of DNA as carrying physical traits like eye color or height. But I believe sonic genetics takes this idea further, extending it to music and sound. Just as phenotypical traits are passed down from one generation to the next, so too are sonic traits – rhythms, melodic structures, vocal techniques, and emotional expressions – woven into the DNA of a people. Music then becomes a living memory of experiences, a way for communities to preserve their stories.

As I continue to explore this idea, I can't ignore the role of trauma and resilience in shaping these sonic patterns. These emotions aren't just felt; they are also expressed and shared. They don't merely inhabit the stories we tell; they also live through the way we create and experience sound. Music becomes a bridge for these emotions to travel across time and space, from one generation to the next.

When I consider the similarities in music across these distant communities, I begin to think that the emotional content of music – shaped by shared experiences like migration, displacement, and survival – may act as a sort of cultural imprint. Music could be a sonic imprint of collective identity that goes beyond specific and local contexts.

This idea also makes me think of epigenetics, the study of how environmental factors influence gene expression. Perhaps there's a parallel to be drawn with sonic genetics. Just as trauma and environment can affect our genes, sound – particularly the rhythmic and emotional patterns passed down through music and the practice and experience of it – may have a similar influence. Could the sonic environment in which a community lives – the music, the rhythms – leave an imprint on how its people express themselves and respond to the world?

As I continue this journey of exploration, I feel a deeper connection to my community, to Suriname, to Indonesia, and to the rhythms that unite us across oceans. There's something profoundly powerful in the idea that our sonic identity isn't just cultural – it's encoded in the very material essence of who we are. Music, in this sense, is not merely a reflection of the past; it's a key to understanding how we carry the memory of those who came before us and how we pass it on.

The concept of sonic genetics challenges the way I think about sound and its role in life, particularly when I consider the development of music in the communities I've explored – Cape Town and Suriname. It's not just about hearing or making music; it's about the possibility that sound and vibration are woven deeply into the cultural fabric of these communities, influencing everything from musical forms to rituals and even social structures. The very rhythms, melodies, and harmonies they've developed may be encoded in their genetic makeup, as if their ability to produce and interpret sound has been passed down as an evolutionary trait.

ARG: And how did those questions and the research relate to the *Invocation #3, Mawali–Taqsim: Improvisation as a Space and Technology of Humanity* that took place in Zanzibar in February 2025? What were the questions you hoped to find answers to during the days you spent among musicians and philosophers? What were the experiences you had there and how did they shape your research for your work featured in Bienal de São Paulo?

TP: To be honest, when I first arrived in Zanzibar, I was pretty confident in my own theories and understanding of sound in the world. And much to my surprise, everything shifted. Just when I thought I had a clearer understanding of what sound really is, I realized I actually don't know as much as I thought! What's really been challenging me is the relationship between time and sound.

Yes, I still believe that sound, music, and rhythm are inherited, but after immersing myself deeply in the intimate relationships people have with their sounds, especially experiencing the powerful ritualistic music of the Sufi community in Zanzibar and feeling the Maloya performance by musicians from Réunion, I came to a surprising conclusion: the sound I've been following around the world seems to have no age. It's a timeless technology. Much like your heartbeat, it's not anchored in a specific time – it's the same today as it was a thousand years ago, and it will still be the same a thousand years in the future. This sound, this rhythm, this pulse is something we need to function in the world – it's not just from the past or for the future, but ever-present.

And now, once again, I find myself completely lost…

ARG: You draw on Sufi rituals and the music thereof, which are rooted in a shared Muslim history of the people in Cape Town, Suriname, and Indonesia. When you speak about a sonic DNA you speak of rhythms that are part of an embodied experience, a collective memory that is activated and made present through its (physical) practice. I see something ritualistic there, a practice of calling spirits from the past and celebrating them in the present – a way of worshipping. This reminds me of the Gnawa tradition, that is also rooted in Sufi tradition, and that has been the focus of our *Invocation* #1 – listening as a practice of coexistence, as well as place- and space-making.

TP: I grew up with Dhikr;[2] it's deeply embedded in our community, family, and personal daily practices. It's not just something we do – it's part of our very existence. Our lives on this earth are spiritual, and Dhikr is a constant thread that connects us to that deeper sense of purpose and connection.

ARG: You said that "the music in these communities doesn't just adapt to circumstances; it resonates with them, shaping the emotional, psychological, and even biological state of the people who create and experience it." Here is where the idea of sonic genetics becomes particularly fascinating: the musical traits that these communities carry forward are not merely cultural symbols; they might also be an evolutionary advantage, a "superpower" passed down through generations. Through music, these communities not only survive, but thrive, tapping into a deep, intrinsic vibrational resonance encoded in their DNA. I wonder if the "superpower" is really the music as such, or rather the practice of it? Isn't it the collective practice of the music, its rhythms, textures, etc., that connects the people with each other in their history and experience of displacement, survival, and cultural transformation that makes it a "superpower" – medium of solidarity?

TP: Yes, I believe it's the practice, but I also think there's something deeper at play. It's the rhythm of our bodies, perhaps a kind of synchronization, that manifests in the sounds we create. These rhythms aren't just about music – they're about how our bodies connect with each other and with our histories. The music, in that sense, becomes an expression of that deeper connection.

BT: Could you comment on how these concepts appear in your current production and whether it relates to the Brazilian context?

TP: In my current production, I explore the role of rhythm, collective practice, and embodied experience in music as tools for connection, survival, and transformation. Music and rhythm, in my work, are more than just sound; they represent a shared experience that binds communities together, especially those shaped by displacement. The rhythms, textures, and collective practices serve as a bridge between past,

53

present, and future, allowing communities to preserve their histories and foster solidarity.

The idea that rhythm and sound are inherent in our bodies, that they're part of our very being, is something I'm investigating further. I focus on how this embodied rhythm becomes a living, breathing expression of survival and resilience. Music is not just heard; it's felt, lived, and passed down as part of our collective memory. It becomes a form of connection that transcends individual experience and evokes something much larger – a shared history and a collective identity.

When I think about Brazil, a country with such rich Afro-Brazilian heritage, these concepts resonate deeply. Many Brazilians have mixed heritage, with roots tracing back to Africa, and this is abundantly evident in their music, particularly in the rhythms that pulse through samba, capoeira, and candomblé. These rhythms, with their strong African roots, are not only musical but also something deeply embedded in the bodies of the people who practice them. The rhythmicality inherent in Brazilian bodies is a direct manifestation of this legacy – one that ties them to a shared history of displacement, survival, and cultural transformation. Much like the communities I work with, the rhythms in Brazil carry the burden of survival and resistance. Music, the practice and the movement with and to it becomes a form of resistance, of recollection, and of recon-nection to a lineage that has been shaped by trauma and resilience. The collective practice of these musical forms fosters unity, allowing people to connect with one another through their shared history and sound. The idea of rhythm as something transmitted through generations, encoded in the very bodies of the people, ties directly into the Brazilian context. It's not just that its music sounds similar to African traditions – it's that the rhythm lives within the people, uniting them across time and space.

So, in my current production, I see these concepts of rhythm, embodiment, and collective practice as universal threads that can be tied to the Brazilian context. The deep connection to African roots, the shared history of displacement, and the resilience of communities through music all converge in both the Brazilian context and the work I've been developing. The rhythms of Brazil, much like the music I'm currently working with, become a testament to survival, solidarity, and the power of collective memory.

> **ET**: In addition to your production, you are actively involved in social and educational projects, debating issues such as racism, Islamophobia and inequality. How do you see the relationship between art, education, and activism, and how do these areas complement each other?

TP: Art and education are fundamentally activism. Both have the power to challenge, inspire, and create change. Art goes beyond aesthetics; it sparks dialogue and exposes injustices, while education empowers people to think critically and act toward social justice. These areas complement each other – art inspires new ideas, education provides the tools to act, and activism drives tangible change. Together, they form a powerful force for addressing issues like racism, Islamophobia, and inequality.

1 Also known as Imam Abdullah Kadi Abdus Salaam, he was a prince from Tidore, an island in eastern Indonesia. Tuan Guru was captured by the Dutch for allegedly conspiring with the British in the context of colonization and banished to the Cape as a prisoner of state. He arrived in April 1780 and was immediately imprisoned on Robben Island, a small island west of Cape Town, where, during his imprisonment, he rewrote the Quran from memory. When he was released in 1793, he wanted to start a Muslim school in Cape Town, which was soon realized: the school was set up in a warehouse on Dorp Street. Two years later, in 1795, he was granted permission to build a mosque. It is now known as the Owwal Mosque, located in Dorp Street, and was the first mosque founded in South Africa.

2 According to Julia Morris, author of the essay "Baay Fall Sufi Da'iras: Voicing Identity Through Acoustic Communities" (*African Arts*, v. 47, no. 1, spring 2014), Dhikr is a form of Islamic worship in which phrases or prayers are repeatedly recited for the purpose of remembering God. It plays a central role in Sufism, and each Sufi order typically adopts a specific Dhikr, accompanied by specific posture, breathing, and movement.

Sonic
Revolution

Thania Petersen

I believe sound exists to bring us together – not just in the way we are
drawn to one another in dance or congregation when we hear music, or how
we gravitate toward birdsong or the hooting of owls hooting, but on a much
deeper, metaphysical level. Sound is more than just noise; it is an inheritance, a thread that connects us not only to each other but to the divine. It
is in that space, in that sound, that we continue to liberate ourselves, redis-
cover who we are, and reconnect with one another. We never feel more
interconnected than when we are fully immersed in the sounds that feel like
home – sounds that anchor us to place, to people, to our shared histories.

This sound is an embodied force carried in our blood, manifesting
in the rhythm with which we move through the world every second of our
lives. Time and space exist only alongside it. Sound lives in every realm of
our society, continually drawing us back to one another, reminding us of
who we are, and where we come from. It is a powerful, ever-present force
that reunites and liberates.

This was exactly my experience in visiting Zanzibar. As children,
we grew up singing certain songs with such devotion and dedication that I
believed they were verses from the Quran. Every Thursday night was dedicated to the recitation and practice of the Ratib al-Haddad and once a year
on the Prophet Muhammad's (SAW)[1] birthday, we would meet to collect
citrus leaves, cut them up, scent them with essential oils and frankincense,
and sing poems of praise all day and night. Only much later did I discover
these were poems and incantations sung for centuries across the Indian
Ocean. These songs were memory banks, repositories of connected times
and people. They embodied gatherings of love and joy. When I delved a bit
deeper into it I learned that one of our most prominent and beloved scholars,
Muhammed Salih Hendricks, had brought these songs/Dhikrs back from
Zanzibar. The connection between Cape Town and Zanzibar, exemplified in
the life of Muhammad Salih Hendricks and other itinerant scholars, speaks
volumes about the powerful role the Indian Ocean played in shaping Islamic
reformist traditions, especially through the Alawī Sufi order. Hendricks,
originally from Swellendam in the Cape, spent 14 years in Mecca before
heading to Zanzibar, where he was appointed a temporary *qāḍī* (judge). His
time there exposed him to Zanzibar's growing emphasis on Sufi practices
and educational reforms – including the promotion of Islamic learning and
the establishment of institutions for women –, all of which would shape his
work when he returned to Cape Town in 1903.

The practice of Dhikr unites the people of Cape Town and
Zanzibar. It is more than a shared spiritual practice; it is a sound, a vibra-
tion, a force that has brought communities together for centuries.
I've always believed sound connects us, not just physically but

communally. This is especially true when it comes to Dhikr. Through it, we reconnect with friendships lost in time but not gone. One of these deep connections is with the Sufi community of Zanzibar, whose practices are woven into the fabric of Cape Town's Islamic life. The Dhikr, carried across the Indian Ocean by figures like Sayyid Muḥsin, Muhammad Salih Hendricks, and others, wasn't just about spiritual growth. It was about building a shared identity – a spiritual and political bond that continues to resonate today.

The sound of Dhikr is a thread that has kept our communities bound together, transcending geography and time. It is an inheritance, a sonic reminder of where we've been and whom we've been with. The Indian Ocean wasn't just a trade route; it was the lifeblood of a network of mystics and teachers, and the Dhikr they carried was its pulse. This pulse ties Zanzibar to Cape Town, creating a shared spiritual heritage that we still carry within us.

What moved me deeply during my presentation was when members of the audience from Zanzibar began singing along to songs I was struggling to play. These were the very songs that had brought me to Zanzibar and ultimately to the island of Tumbatu on my final day – a closed Sufi community where foreigners are not allowed. Yet, again, the Dhikr opened doors. As if time had dissolved, it allowed me into this sacred island, the heart of Zanzibar's Sufi tradition, where we sang together once more. It was a powerful act of reunification, an experience that transcended time.

I was overwhelmed by the realization that time plays no role in how this music exists in the world. It still confounds me, but I came to understand that this music is like our heartbeat – it doesn't age. It is the rhythm of our lives, sustaining us, keeping us alive. It functions now as it did a century ago and will do a century from now. Even if no one from my community visits this place for another hundred years, when – or rather if – one day my great-great-great-granddaughter sets foot on that soil, drawn by the same song, it will feel as if no time has passed between us.

Sonic Genetics as a Spiritual Force for Unity

When considering sonic genetics from a metaphysical and spiritual perspective, one might view sound as more than just a tool for communication; rather, it may be seen as a way that our ancestors ensured we would always find our way back to one another, no matter how separated we became.

Sound, as I see it, carries a deep spiritual memory – a language encoded into the very fabric of existence that transcends time and space. This spiritual imprint is passed down through generations in music, rhythm, and melody. Sonic genetics, in this light, becomes a key to reconnecting us to each other, regardless of the cultural, geographic, or political boundaries that divide us. It is the universal, unseen thread that binds us, guiding us back to our shared humanity.

A Metaphysical Anti-Apartheid System

I propose that sonic genetics can be seen as an inherent counterforce to the divisions created by colonialism, apartheid, and other systens of violence. In a metaphysical sense, sound – particularly music – functions as a kind of anti-apartheid system, opposing the forces that fragment and isolate us.

Colonialism and apartheid are historical forces sought to artificially divide us through race, culture, and geography. These systems fractured communities, severed connections, and erased cultural identities. But sound, music, and rhythm – rooted in the very DNA of the oppressed – persisted, even in the face of violence. They were resistance; an audible rebellion against division.

As a *language for unit*, this sonic genetic language may be our most powerful tool for resisting separation. It bypasses the spoken word, speaking directly to our collective spirit. Music, in this sense, is an ancestral message – a reminder that no matter how history tries to divide us, shared experiences, rhythms, and emotions will always draw us back together.

The Sonic Resistance to Cultural Erasure

Faced with cultural erasure – through colonization, slavery, or apartheid – sound has served as cultural survival. It is as if the very essence of who we are, as human beings, cannot be fully eradicated. Despite efforts to suppress, divide, and destroy, the rhythms of our ancestors echo through time.

This sonic resistance is more than cultural preservation; it is a spiritual assertion of identity and power. The drumbeat, the call-and-response, the harmonies of traditional music – all are part of a larger metaphysical system that continually reaffirms our shared existence, struggle, and capacity for joy, love, and healing.

Bringing Us Back to Each Other

Ultimately, sonic genetics offers a path back to one another, however distant we may be – physically, emotionally, or socially. Music and sound breaks through the boundaries imposed by colonialism, apartheid, and other forms of violence. They are both remembrance and spiritual unity.

It is as if our ancestors embedded a secret language in music, a timeless call urging us to reunite. When we hear these sounds, when we feel these rhythms, we are not merely experiencing music – we are reconnecting with ancestral souls, shared heritage, and the emotional DNA of our people.

Through sound's vibrations, we can transcend division and return to the collective understanding that we are, always, connected, that our struggles, triumphs, and identities are shared in the most profound, metaphysical way.

Sonic Genetics Not as a Metaphor but Actually Inherited and Encoded in Our Biological DNA

A study examining the genetic basis for beat synchronization – the ability to move or perceive a musical beat in sync with others – analyzed 606,825 individuals and identified 69 genetic regions linked to this trait.

The research shows that beat synchronization is associated with motor function, breathing, processing speed, and chronotype, suggesting a shared genetic basis. Rhythm perception and synchronization play a crucial role in human experiences, influencing communication, social behavior, and cognition. In essence, the study explores how genetics and biology shape our sense of rhythm and how it impacts our cognitive and social lives.

Additionally, the study found that beat synchronization was genetically related to other traits associated with biological rhythms, such as breathing, walking speed, and chronotype. This phenomenon, known as pleiotropy – where a single genetic variant affects multiple traits –, suggests a deeper biological connection between rhythm and bodily functions. This indicates that rhythm is not merely aesthetic but integral to our bodily systems.

A Sonic Revolution

In conclusion, I believe sonic genetics may hold the key to collective healing, unity, and spiritual revolution. By reconnecting with the sounds and rhythms that our ancestors passed down, we can dismantle the walls built by colonialism and apartheid. We can heed the call to come together and rebuild a world without divisions.

Sound is more than art – it is a living force that connects us to one another, to the past, and the spiritual forces of resistance running through our blood. Through sound, we always find our way back to each other.

60

1   Abbreviation of "Sallallahu Alayhi wa Sallam" [Peace and blessings of God be upon him].

The Dhow Countries Music Academy of Zanzibar

Halda Mohamed Alkanaan

The Dhow Countries Music Academy Zanzibar (DCMA) is a non-profit, non-governmental organization officially registered in March 2001. As the first and only music academy in Zanzibar, DCMA provides music education to individuals interested in learning both traditional and contemporary music styles, alongside instrumental training. The academy operates on the principle of making music education accessible to all, offering lessons at minimal cost. It places strong emphasis on preserving and promoting Zanzibar's rich musical heritage, including iconic styles such as Taarab, Beni, and Kidumbak. By providing high-quality instruction, DCMA aims to nurture talent, creativity, and professional musicianship among Zanzibar's emerging artists and cultural practitioners.

The academy's programs are designed to foster a deep appreciation for music, encourage the preservation of Zanzibar's cultural heritage, and equip students with the skills necessary to build sustainable careers in the music industry.

Core Components of DCMA

DCMA comprises a variety of programs and initiatives tailored to meet the diverse needs of music learners and the broader cultural community:

- Music lessons in various instruments, including violin, oud, qanun, cello, guitar, percussion, zumari, accordion, piano, and others.
- Student scholarship program to support talented students from underprivileged backgrounds.
- Music library offering instruments, audiovisual materials, books, and other educational resources for all members.
- Music agency to promote Zanzibari musicians, facilitating local, regional, and international performance opportunities.
- Schools Program to introduce music education in public and private schools, identify young talents, and promote cultural awareness.
- Children and youth program to foster creativity and artistic expression as part of child development.
- Rural outreach program, bringing music education and instrument training to villages outside Zanzibar's urban centers in Unguja and Pemba. Currently, DCMA operates a fully functional branch in Mahonda.
- Workshops, master classes and seminars held both locally and internationally, exposing musicians to diverse music styles and enhancing their skills.
- Student exchange program, facilitating cultural and educational exchanges locally and internationally.

→ Capacity building, focusing on improving the teaching and administrative competencies of DCMA's staff.

Vision and Mission

Our Vision:
To be recognized as the leading internationally accredited center for traditional music education in East and Central Africa, while fostering the appreciation of traditional and contemporary music as a catalyst for cultural and economic development.

Our Mission:
DCMA is committed to playing a pivotal role in strengthening the music industry in Zanzibar by focusing on research, training, promotion, preservation, and development of the musical heritage of Zanzibar and the Dhow region. Through structured education, performance opportunities, and cross-cultural collaborations, DCMA seeks to empower musicians and enrich Zanzibar's musical landscape.

Aims and Objectives

DCMA operates with the following primary aims and objectives:

→ To provide music education opportunities to Zanzibari residents, with particular emphasis on young people, children, and women, ensuring the preservation of traditional music.
→ To professionally train musicians through structured courses, seminars, workshops, research, and debates.
→ To equip talented musicians with skills and resources needed to establish sustainable careers in music.
→ To expand employment opportunities in Zanzibar's music industry by marketing and promoting local musicians for performances at local venues, regional festivals, and international events.
→ To enhance international collaboration, fostering communication, networking, and cultural diplomacy among countries in the Dhow region (Africa, India, Pakistan, Indonesia, the Indian Ocean Islands, and the Arabian Peninsula). To establish strong cultural and educational partnerships with local, regional, and international organizations, fostering an environment of mutual respect, equality, and tolerance.

64

- Expand educational programs: Broaden and diversify the curriculum to incorporate a wide range of musical styles and techniques, integrating both traditional and contemporary approaches.
- Strengthen community outreach: Develop initiatives that engage the local community through workshops, concerts, and collaborative projects.
- Build international partnerships: Foster connections with global institutions and musicians to encourage cultural exchange and collaborative opportunities.
- Enhance facilities and resources: Invest in state-of-the-art facilities and learning resources to support educational and performance activities, in a creative, conducive environment.

Administrative Structure of DCMA

DCMA is governed by a Board of Directors comprising professionals from diverse local and international backgrounds. The academy operates with an efficient team led by a CEO and structured into education and administrative divisions.

Education Team:
- Artistic Director
- Academic Director
- 3 Full-Time Teachers (All Tanzanian)
- 9 Part-Time Teachers (All Tanzanian)

Administrative Team:
- Managing Director (Female Tanzanian)
- Accounts Officer (Male Tanzanian)
- Communications Officer (Male Tanzanian)
- Librarian (Female Tanzanian)
- Care Taker (Female Tanzanian)

Activities

Since its opening in September 2002, DCMA has gained local and international recognition as a center of cultural excellence under the motto: "Music for Education, Music for Employment, Music for Enjoyment."

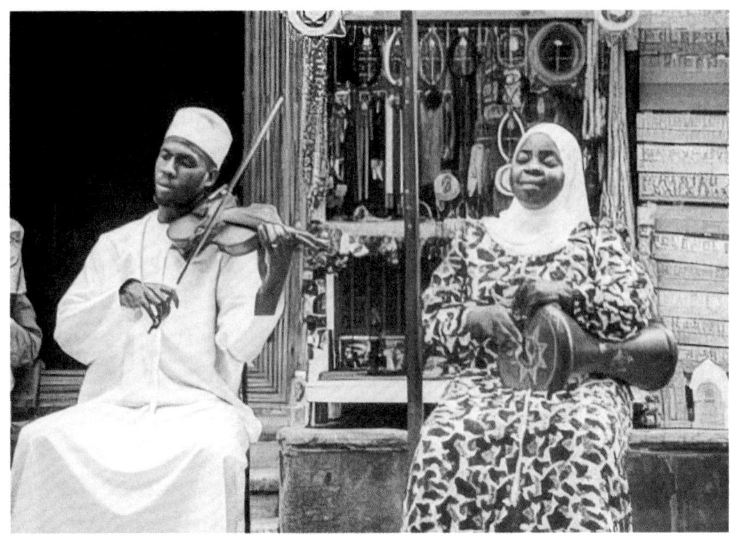

© Sauti Za Busara, 2025.

Music for Education

DCMA delivers high-quality training in instrumental performance and music theory, offering workshops and master classes. To date, DCMA has trained over 3,200 students and hosted numerous international workshops. The academy also maintains a small music museum and archive, offering insights into the history of Taarab music, its instruments and legendary artists.

Music for Employment

Many DCMA alumni and faculty members pursue professional careers in music. Notably:

→   75% of Zanzibar's top-performing musicians are DCMA graduates.
→   90% of DCMA's teachers are alumni of the academy.
→   Graduates often participate in recordings, cultural exchanges, and international performances.

Music for Enjoyment

DCMA frequently organizes performances that bring traditional and contemporary music to local audiences.

Curriculum

The academic year at DCMA is divided into two semesters, scheduled around the Muslim holy month of Ramadan.

DCMA offers structured music education through the following programs:

+ Certificate Program: A three-year structured course that includes assessments and performance opportunities.
+ Diploma Program: Intended for advanced students and educators, offering pathways to higher education. (Currently on hold due to financial constraints.)
+ Additionally, specialized short-term training is available for individuals or international students by arrangement.

Awards and Recognition

DCMA's contribution to music education and cultural preservation has earned several accolades:

+ U.S. Ambassador's Award for Cultural Preservation (2002).
+ Zanzibar Music Award for Contribution to Music Development (2007).
+ Tigo Zanzibar Music Award (2008).
+ Zanzibar Music Award for Preserving Traditional Music.
+ Roskilde World Music Award recognized for teaching traditions (2010).

DCMA
Young Stars

The DCMA Young Stars is a dynamic ensemble of thirteen talented students dedicated to preserving and celebrating the rich musical traditions of Zanzibar. As emerging artists from the Dhow Countries Music Academy (DCMA), they bring a fresh vitality to Taarab, a genre deeply rooted in the island's cultural heritage.

Blending traditional and contemporary influences, the Young Stars captivate audiences with their performances, showcasing the beauty of Zanzibari music through a diverse array of instruments, including the violin, qanun, clarinet, bongos, tabla, and powerful vocals. Their performances transport audiences through the evocative melodies and rhythms that have defined Taarab for generations.

With passion, artistry, and dedication, the DCMA Young Stars embody the future of musical excellence, ensuring that the treasured sounds of Zanzibar continue to resonate and evolve for generations to come.

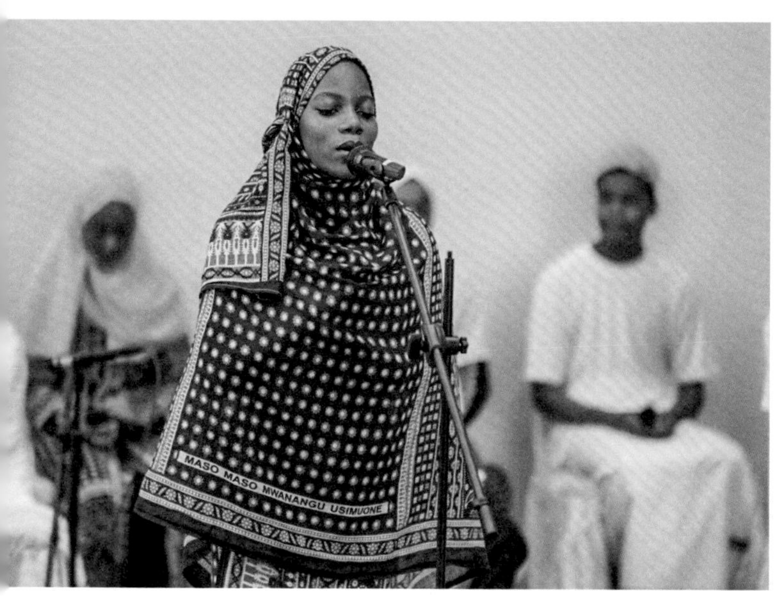

Performance
documentation

Writing the Sound of Zanzibar

Thabit Omar Kiringe

I joined the Dhow Countries Music Academy (DCMA) in 2002 as a music theory teacher. But perhaps I should take you back to the years of the Father of the Nation[1] and the experience that led me to work with Taarab music.

While visiting the State House, Modibo Keïta (1915-1977), the president of Mali, came to Tanzania. That night, we were invited to a function in his honor, where the police band was scheduled to perform. By that time, the bandmasters used to perform music by Beethoven, Tchaikovsky, and many other foreign composers. So, one officer approached the bandmaster and said, "the guests want to hear traditional music from Tanzania." From that time, my mind opened. It was as if somebody took something out of me. And I said to myself: well, at home we have some Taarab music. If only it were written down, we could perform it. So that's when I had the desire to write Taarab. And my very first song was "Nanasi," translating as "pineapple." It was 1973, before most of you were born. And that's when I wrote my first Taarab song.

Now, let me speak about the importance of Taarab for Zanzibar. Especially the Zanzibari Taarab. It is not a mere pastime. We met very humble Zanzibaris. They're very quiet, silent, and it's peaceful here because of our culture, the Taarab culture. We hate quarrels, and so does Taarab. Taarab brought us up. It raised us. Our country is a blend of different Taarabs. Because Taarab was born in an Arabian place, but it had some Indians, and then today we have this blend that is the Zanzibari Taarab.

Taarab is very important, especially to this generation. Taarab is so good. Back then, you did not dance Taarab. You would sit and listen to this prestigious music. Different from now. I would take my wife, we would go out, and sit and listen to music. And if you would wake up from your seat, you were going to give the singers a gift. And it was respect. Yeah, awarding these artists without showing any disobedience.

Now I'll talk about improvisation. This improvisation, some just hear it: "*taqsim, taqsim…*" [improvise, improvise…]. But I would like us to listen to two improvisations, and so we could understand how the Zanzibarians are through these two different *taqsims*. Let's have a listen. [Song is played.] This improvisation was done directly by the singer. In improvisations, you express yourself how you feel, how you want to play your instrument. If you have a conducting band, you just let the band do whatever they want. That's the meaning of improvisation. There are other taqsims that are received by the singer, and other improvisations.

This song is called "Cheo Chako" [a song by Rukia Ramadhani]. I was given this job by the State House. And the state house wanted this song to be played by a police band there. But instead of playing "Cheo Chako," they just played "Cheo Chango." They played it differently but had the same song. So we are not sure, but someone who came wanted to hear this song titled "Cheo Chako."

Then I will play it a little bit. And I want you to listen to how the singing is received by the keyboard players. [Song is played.] You can see that the first improvisation is so different from this one. The first improvisation has its own sentimental feelings, it expresses the sadness of someone. If you had problems back home, when you come to listen to this improvisation, you might find yourself coming to tears. The song was performed directly by the artist. But the second one, there is a small bridge that is normally brought up by the keyboards. And then the singer follows. So, the taste is different. And the value is the music. It makes the music feel real and nice. Whether you want it or not, you will enjoy it. That's improvisation. That's the meaning. And its importance. It makes something beautiful. Especially Taarab.

Not every song has improvisation. Some others don't. They just start straightforwardly. But if you look deep inside, the second one has a different improvisation within. And I will not explain that. It will take a long time. So, it starts with improvisation, instrumental improvisation. After that, Ms. Rukia [Ramadhani] comes and sings. And then music comes. And then there is another improvisation that takes you from one place to another. Thus, it makes a shift of emotions.

Now let me talk about the importance of notations. Especially in our Taarab music. Why is it important? I've tried to look for many songs, especially one known as "Karata" by Khadija Salim. I've really searched for it. I haven't found it anywhere. There are many traditional songs that are lost because they were not written. There are some tape records, flashes, CDs. But our traditional songs, most of them we do not have. If you happen to hear it somewhere, you wonder. But now, songs like "Cheo Chako," Madam Halda called me, with my fellow artistic director, and advised us: why don't we write a book with notations on traditional Taarab music? It was good advice because we are here and we are all capable of writing these songs. My capability is his capability. Tryphon Evarist has written almost fifty songs, because he writes with a laptop. I write by hand, and I have almost thirty songs. In total we have almost eighty songs that have been written in the form of notation. If you take that anywhere, then you will see the Zanzibari. When hear that improvisation, if you're in China, if you're anywhere, as long as you see it because of that notation, then you will feel the Zanzibari feeling. It's very important for memory and preservation.

For those of us who started back then, we used to play Beethoven. I didn't know them, but I just enjoyed playing that music by Beethoven and Tchaikovsky. But we have our songs. We have our fathers, who are not here today. And how are we going to remember them? Because if you write the song, you also write who sang it, who composed it, who played it, maybe Nad Ikwaan Safaa. All the writings are there. And those writings will be there forever. The writer is Saif Salim. It will be known. And if Saif Salim sang it, it would be known in that book. So, it will stay there forever. These songs will never be forgotten because of these notations. They will be read and be read by several generations that are coming.

Now on challenges, there's a bit of a challenge here. Sometimes I do laugh at myself while I'm writing. Because these old players never used notations. Especially the military bands. If they had eight clarinets, then all eight clarinets played the same tune. But these local groups that had no knowledge of notations, whoever went to teach them would hear different tunes from each clarinet players. Because the ear training was so different. Whoever hears and plays does something different from what is conducted by the leader. So, you come to the next day, after the first day of practice, and you hear something different from what happened. Because the songs have keys.

So, the local players have a different ear training, which is very difficult. Maybe I could remind something about these verses. Back then, we were given, five people, one song to write. Then the bandmaster from Moshi came and found that these five people who were writing the same song. And he said to the bandmaster, Mwagilo: "Don't allow these students to write the same song. Everyone has his or her own ear." But the bandmaster said: "I don't want you to write me the music. I want you to write me the verses." I won't remember them, but I remember one of the verses, "Africa, a great nation of importance…" There are more words that continue. But among us five people, one did not write "Africa, a great nation of importance…" He wrote something else. Because the ear differs. So, there is a challenge for our keyboard players and violinists. Some play a different tune and others play another tune. For us, as writers, we hear. And we try to see which one is perfect and which one is truthful. And that's what you take note of. You come to rest when the singer starts singing. But the keyboards are very challenging to document, because they play without notation. So, if you ask: "What key are you playing this song in?" I just say: "I just start with Re." It starts with a D. But D, is it on which key? In C major it's Re, but in F major, D is La. At first, I really struggled, especially with Matona [Mohamed Issa Haji]. We struggled because he says it's starting with Sol, but on C major, Sol is G. But for F major, G is La. So, you see? If you're writing that song, there are things that you have to adjust so

73   that you understand that this song begins with a certain key and follows that. Some others play with an F sharp, others do a F flat.

So, if you have a keyboard and you play two keys at the same time, it confuses you. Its sound is so different. It doesn't work because you simply distorts the whole thing. We do face that.

And also, there is a tendency of rewinding. You must have a proper ear and there is no one to disturb you. At home you must stop everything. I normally lock my door because I don't want anyone to disturb me. My children know me, they know that if I have my keyboard there, I don't want anyone to ask me or say something to me from morning to afternoon.

And the other challenge is the equipment itself. Like me, I need a laptop so that I can write my music so fast. But if I show you the things I've written by hand, you'll be surprised. One of them is this book [shows a book]. As you can see, this is handwritten. One is complete and I've given it to Madam Halda to restore it. Even the song "Cheo Chako" is in here. And I'm sure also the song "Kijiti" is here. And this is the second book. One is complete and this is the second one. The first one has twenty songs of traditional Taarab. I do not write the modern songs. I write the traditional Taarab. That's what I want, because we need to preserve it for the next generation. Because the next generation will go astray. This modern Taarab will be seen as Taarab, and the traditional Taarab will not be known. It will be considered as the oldest music. And they won't want us anymore. Because modern Taarab will be taking us astray. So it's important for us to document the traditional Taarab.

I really appreciate Madam Halda's efforts in making us document these songs. And we have started. It's a memory for the future. I can say Swahili is the seventh language in the world. And here you'll find the songs written in Swahili in these books Notations and the lyrics are there. They won't lose anything, whoever will come in the future. Even if they sing differently, I'm sure that these books will get it into universality. There won't be a reason for them to sing or play it differently. We're sure that these books will get all over Africa and all over the world.

I was training a certain Japanese and I asked him: "Where did you learn Swahili?" He said: "I learned it in Japan." He's Japanese, but he studied Swahili in Japan. And today we're looking at Arabian, Indian and European movies and they're all in Swahili. Why don't we send them Swahili songs if they can make Swahili movies? And that's the importance of notation of Taarab music. It's a challenge.

My advice to my fellow parents: music is not something illicit. Let's encourage our children to study music. Let's not hinder them. Because I didn't grow up to be a hooligan. For thirty years, until now I'm 70, I'm with my dignity. Why am I not a hooligan? Hooliganism is within someone's own behavior. So, let's allow our children to come and study music. We have little children who sing Taarab through notations. They play keyboards through notations. They're very young, under 20 years old. And they play keyboards. They sing with notations. They play with notations. We do not deny them to try as our old men did with us, because our old men used to cram it. So, we teach them anything, like to adapt and also to play the notes. Some have been studying it for one year but you might think they have done it for six years.

My last thoughts are for those who have a will to help us, who wish to help us. We are struggling with our location. We are always shifting from place to place. So we really need your help. For those who are capable of providing us with a proper large house, our school is struggling. We are training people from Arusha, Moshi, and different parts of Tanzania. They're studying. They hear us on social media, newspapers. They go to Dar es Salaam and they look for us. In Bagamoyo there is a music school, but once they get a diploma there, they are told : "If you want an actual musical career, you should go and study in Zanzibar." After having a diploma there, if you want to develop true talent, you must come here. So, if they have a diploma there, they come here and start as a third-grade student, because here's where professionalism is. So, we really need your help. We are struggling in this special space. For those who are capable please help us secure a proper facility [round of applause].

1   Reference to Abeid Karume (1905-1972), Zanzibar's first president after the Zanzibar Revolution (started on January 12, 1964), which overthrew the sultan and put an end to almost three centuries of Arab rule, transferring power to the island's Africans.

Taarab

Ajítẹnà Marco Scarassatti

The sound of rain sheltered us
surroundings...
On top of that we call stage
there we all sat, each one with their instrument
in the time of latency preceding the first gesture.
Gestating the sound that'll erupt from silence.
In an even smaller fraction of that time, the Sufi poet crossed my mind.
Music lies in silence.
Silence,
said Smetak,
sound is born from silence's densification.
Awaiting,
feeling like a lonely one in a crowd
the sound of rain turned blurry and distant...
I wielded the bow, I placed it on the string of the invented instrument
Cocho-Bird, a Ìyàmi who sings with her exposed vocal chords.
A mother, a seed bearer, who remakes the path of creation.
I pressed the tip of the bow on the string, not making a sound yet.
On the brink of the first note,
Monk's piano, drew a spiral
And, in this space-time
spinned Coleman, Parker, Monk, Matana, Coltrane,
Taylor
and so many others
who sounded the spirit of freedom
subverting all the colonizing instruments.
Pure incantation, they turned into companion species.
And just like rain, their thoughts flew so very far away
vissungos, repentes, and *emboladas* still resonating,
silence got denser.
I, too, was the tip of the bow putting pressure on the string,
dwelling in that point of contact.
I escaped and became string,
pitching myself, shaped as sound-soul
and gesture.
I soared!
Vibrant among other souls,
I wasn't even sound,
I just soared
and listened.
Pause!

Noises of bliss and sorrow
whistled.
Irradiating, spinning around.
Magnetizing
the acoustics of the place,
a *terreiro*;
mingle with the dream.
They, too, dream…
In a random corner of this crossroad,
Unafraid,
an asleep transitioned body awaits,
breathes
listens to dreams
of its living death.
It rises.
Eyes wide open,
awakened!
Perceiving the place,
While its skin undulates with winged vibrations.
While it smells and tastes the earth.
While its tongue touches the air.
the Body,
is nameless here,
so it can be many, multiple, manifold
myriadxxxxxxxxxx*HAUX*xxxxxxxxxxxxxxx*iiiiiiiiiiiii*
And into its auricula,
the master of chants blows.
Rise up!
Listen to the silence for a while,
until the Iroke strikes.
In the back of the room,
rings a thread
Diriguiridiriguiridiriguiri Diriguiridiriguiridiriguiri
Diriguiridiriguiridiriguiri…
It rings and strikes the sacred handbell's carved
wood.
Irradiating, vibrating, in quick pulses, strident impulses.
Magnetizing. The body is the place,
it feels its percussed skin,
a fold.

In each pore it touches,
the beat moves.
Noises of bliss and sorrow soar like spirits,
spreading transcendences into the Orí.
Unexpected, the arrival of a new rhythm
bordered by the clinkings of *platinelas*,[1]
leaps and loosens
with every beat of a rebana
Túndek tekdún tek Dúndek tekdún tek Dúndek tekdún tek Dúndek tekdún
tek...
And in the off-beats, they alternate
at the sharp touch of the skin,
at the border
térun téréruntérérun térun térun téréruntérérun térun térun,
téréruntérérun
the percussed skin,
in motion.
It crosses the labyrinth
The body is the place. Lifting its shoulders
projecting the sternum forward
in an impulse.
Again!
Feeling it!
It ser-pen-tines
moves the lower back
bending over thighs and knees
walking as two, swaying
Feet walking
forward, backward
kan k kankan k kan k kankan k kan k kankan k...
The gan marks it
Ògún's orín
contrasting with the low tom's sound
which beats as it loosens and floats
as it shakes the ground
TUM Dak daK TUM DaK
TUM Dak daK TUM
TUM Dak daK TUM DaK
TUM Dak daK TUM

The body dances and in its dance
the blend is sorted out.
Listening improvises
it opens a rift in the present
it deepens.
Interregnum,
breathing gasps.
Taking up space
it moves across the labyrinth.
Breathing is the bellows that blows
a continuous quartal chord, contiguous with the skin
hands shaking
xhaque xhaquerê xhaque xhaquerê xhaque xhaquerê xhaque xhaquerê
xhaque xhaquerê xhaque xhaquerê
dancing
and in its dance
the blend is sorted out
The body is the place,
it feels its percussed skin,
each pore touched
by the beat moves.
a *Tá Ga dún Tá Ga dúnTá Ga dúnTá Ga dúnTá Ga dún* cuts across
distancing itself.
Listening to a prose
on the bellows
inhaling, lifting its shoulders,
exhaling, eyelids
closed, breathing.
The Lúna's beat talks to a Taqsim
Caxixi, Berimbau, Kithara
pierce and percuss, resonating their strings in the terreiro's chants.
Even if all chants are whirlwinds of
every presented sound
listen to the wind, a short displacement,
scraped by hands on the Ṣẹ kẹ rẹ .
The body spins over its feet
it opens a rift
in listening, the Interregnum
deepens
breathing gasps
The Orí is the place

the *terreiro* moves,
reveries.
Noises of bliss and sorrow settle
becoming the clay of the ground, of the floor where we dance.
Becoming dance,
the dance-body of visiting sounds
and in its dance
the blend is sorted out
they find, they improvise a path.
The practice of common making
the practice
of the ordinary
the practice
of becoming,
after a lot of dancing
one notices, the body
shrinks.
As if in a spiral, fitting and dwelling
in the auricula,
and entering the labyrinth,
to find
itself
and unravelled from there
taking over all the space
with its voice.
Thrilled as it chants a melisma
Ya Layl Ya 'Ayn
improvising
intuiting
an existence
deepening present time
a dance that soars subtly like mist
travels through the akasha
txschíuuuuuuúúúúúiiiiiiiiiiiiiuuuuuuoooooooooôôôôôô
whistling *siuxiiiiiiiiiiieouu*
interreign
imprecise
intuitive
to whom the soul has chosen to be
to sur-vi-ve
where the soul lives, a finger touches the string

loosening
displacing, the soul
whistles
the soul travels as sound…
Kakakiriká!
It's the sound of the gourd
the shekere's gourd.
It was split
by the very tools it carried
when it got to Aye
but the gourd is a seed bearer.
As one, I am many!
becoming, would've been,
the zen
boatwoman,
facing a gigantic wave
I steer my boat-body a/way as if through a blooming garden
I dance in its transcendental
undulation
I dance with all of them who leave
beneath the clay of the ground where we dance
a ritual
I'm tongue and I dare touching
the air
I'm tongue and I dare
language
I breathe the verse
I listen to the silent chant, my Orí
whistles
intuits
improvises
interreigns
imprecise
here the body has a name
collective Orí
by Ajalá's hands
from where I chose to be.
Improvising is
the song of an imagined world
a crossroad song
a gourd that splits

kakakirka.
In seedbeds
so there can be many, multiple, manifold, myriads
improvisation like a collective Orí.
I'm collective, joined, contiguous with a beaten ground,
even it the ground-chants are spiral windwhirls –
I spin unafraid
my feet mark the floor
I hear a low, hoarse, whispered chant
a spell
Ọfọ̀
and the
plucking of an Iganga
the terreiro becomes empty
the plucking of an Iganga
empties
a spell
Ọfọ̀
noises,
of bliss and sorrow?
… a terreiro
…the sounds blend together,
walking through the acoustic space, ether, as if crossing from one
riverbank to another,
along a path of stones.
These stones disintegrate, one by one, as soon as they're touched by the feet
crossing them,
Repetition
as an orbital gesture
Earth spins,
sounding the spirit of freedom
the unforeseen
to claim the instruments,
companion species
improvising silences,
whistling
irradiating as sound,
twirling
the acoustics of a place,
terreiro;
Unafraid

83

in a corner.
Asleep it awaits,
ears opening!
awaking
whistling
Magnetizing
the space,
words, sounds
a screaming silence.
To the ears,
the sounds arise from Earth, they rise like waves
climbing feet…
until they rattle the braid
The ear is a body
in a conch,
the blend is sorted out
it dances
they find, they improvise a path.
Becoming, would've been
dwell
in impossibility.
When the Orí work simultaneously,
it's a *free-verse* composition
… running like the waters of a river
as one who crosses from one riverbank to another,
through a path of stones.
The waters preserve the river and its name, and constantly baptize it…
unforeseen, intuition, improvisation
… volatile
time …
tempo
unexpected(ly)
opens a rift
in the present
intuiting
deepening
interreigning
breathing gasps
Taking up space
improvising
crossing

Breathing is the bellows that blows
body, weather,
dreaming
relentlessly.
Whatever it is you see,
don't settle
don't announce it as new.
Being the instant,
being the intuitive instance
holding the shadow of a fish on the surface of a river
as one who crosses from one riverbank to another,
along a path of stones.
The waters preserve the river, constantly…
the waters are always new
the river remains the same.
The waters, the river
tomorrow is never
between what happened, be/coming, and what's yet to come
a body between riverbanks.
Creating things they can't steal from us!
The instant!
Don't settle and don't announce it as new.
The waters are always new, though the river remains the same.
The waters constantly baptize it…
With every current tongue intertwining
the trans-idiomatic body
awakens,
perceiving the place,
its skin ripples with winged vibrations,
smelling and tasting the earth.
Its tongue touches the air.
The Body,
is nameless here,
so that, in be/coming, there may be
noises of bliss and sorrow,
whistling through a clay bottle.
All sonority fits within,
it twirls.
Amidst the sonorities of our surroundings
children, small screams, crickets, stirrings
breathing through the clay bottle, wind through the window crack

Magnetizing
Together
Dreaming, unafraid,
the terreiro's music.
All of them meet, all of them touch, all of them touch the terreiro
in a corner an asleep body
breathes
listening to dreams
eyes wide open!
Finding itself on the other shore
It pauses.
Inhaling, lifting its shoulders
exhaling, eyelids
closed, breathing
breathing
breathing
breathing
listening to the silence
the Iroke strikes far
it rings a metal
thread
striking the sacred handbell's carved wood
distancing itself
inhaling, lifting its shoulders
diriguiridiriguiridiriguiridiriguiri...
exhaling, eyelids
closed. Breathes
breathes
pauses
the sounds that were just experienced,
now disperse.
We look at each other,
accomplices in ecstasy, recognizing each other
embracing
our eyelids close our eyes,
but not our ears
the rain sheltered us
applauded us.

The Art of Taarab Poetry and Music Composition

Mohamed Ilyas

It is both an honor and a privilege to stand before you today at the 36th Bienal de São Paulo – *Invocation* #3 Zanzibar, and to share a subject that is deeply intertwined with my life: Taarab music and poetry. Through this presentation, I invite you into the world of Taarab not merely as a musical genre, but as a profound art form – one of storytelling, improvisation, and cultural expression – that has been at the heart of Zanzibar's identity for centuries.

Taarab is more than just entertainment; it is poetry set to melody, a dialogue between the artist and the audience, a means of expressing emotions, history, and social realities through carefully crafted verses. My own journey with Taarab began with my passion for composing lyrics and crafting melodies that do more than entertain – they carry meaning and move hearts.

Understanding the Essence of Taarab

Taarab music is rooted in the rich cultural tapestry of Zanzibar, where African, Arabic, Persian, and Indian influences merge to create a unique and expressive musical tradition. Its origins date back to the late 19th century, when Sultan Barghash bin Said introduced it to Zanzibar after being inspired by the classical Arabic and Egyptian music he encountered during his travels. Over the years, Zanzibar developed its own distinct style of Taarab, making it a deeply rooted tradition that resonates with the everyday experiences of its people.

At its core, Taarab is an art of expression – a way for the singer and composer to channel emotion, social reflection, and personal insight through poetic verse. The lyrics are often metaphorical, layered with meaning, and serve as a medium for expressing love, longing, joy, sorrow, and even nuanced political commentary.

Audience interaction is one of Taarab's defining features. The singer does not merely perform but engages in a dynamic call-and-response interplay with the audience, who in turn interpret the lyrics through the lens of their own lived experiences.

The Power of Words in Taarab Poetry

In Taarab, the words are as important as the melody – if not more so. A well-crafted Taarab song is imbued with deep poetic symbolism, often employing metaphors and allegories to convey complex emotions. Some songs celebrate love and passion, while others subtly critique societal norms, injustice, or political realities.

As a composer and lyricist, I strive to craft words that resonate with listeners' emotions. The beauty of Taarab poetry lies in its openness to interpretation – each listener may derive a different meaning, making the experience intimate and deeply personal.

Taarab lyrics often feature: *romanticism and love*, expressing devotion, admiration, and the pain of unrequited love; *philosophy and wisdom*, offering reflections on life, fate, and the human experience; *social commentary*, addressing issues of morality, class, and cultural changes; and *playfulness and humor*, using clever wordplay and double meanings to entertain audiences.

This poetic richness is what gives Taarab is timeless appeal, enabling it to resonate across generations.

The Role of Improvisation in Taarab

One of the key elements that sets Taarab apart from other music traditions is improvisation. While its compositions follow structured verses and melodies, Taarab always leave room for artists to transcend the written form – offering space for personal expression, emotional depth, and spontaneous engagement with the audience.

Improvisation in music is the space in which one allows oneself to go off script, to express deeper truths than those prescribed, and to convey emotions, political views, and personal messages beyond what is formally notated – both literally and metaphorically. It is a space for a different kind of communication between performer and listener, where feeling takes precedence over form.

This improvisational aspect of Taarab makes every performance unique. No two renditions are ever identical, as the singer feeds off the energy of the audience, the mood of the moment, and the emotional weight of the lyrics. This spontaneous, raw expression is what makes Taarab such a human and intimate art form.

My Journey in Taarab Music

My personal journey in Taarab has been a lifelong passion that began at a young age. I first joined Nadi Ikhwan Safaa, Zanzibar's oldest Taarab group, where I developed my skills as both a composer and performer. Over time, my desire to experiment and push creative boundaries led me to travel to Dar es Salaam, where I joined Al-Watan, one of the most influential Taarab groups of the time. During this period, I not only refined my musical abilities but also expanded my knowledge of composition, instrumentation, and lyrical poetry. I also had the honor of joining the Tanzanian Police Band, where I further developed my musicianship and explored different influences.

One of the highlights of my career was composing and recording songs dedicated to Queen Elizabeth II, which earned a personal letter of gratitude from Her Majesty. This

91

moment reinforced my belief in the power of music as a universal language that transcends cultural and geographic boundaries.

Throughout my career, I have remained committed to the evolution of Taarab – to honoring its legacy while guiding it toward the future. I have collaborated with many artists, mentored younger generations, and dedicated myself to preserving this tradition through both innovation and education.

The Importance of Notation in Preserving Taarab

One of the greatest challenges we face today is the preservation of Taarab music. Traditionally, much of the music has been passed down orally, which places it at risk of being lost over time. Without written notation, many compositions may vanish with the passing of elder generations.

This is why music notation is crucial. By transcribing Taarab compositions into written scores, we: preserve traditional melodies and lyrics for future generations; enable faithful reproduction of classic compositions; provide opportunities for musicians worldwide to learn and perform Taarab; and ensure that improvisation remains a choice rather than a necessity resulting from forgotten melodies.

By documenting and archiving these compositions, we can safeguard the future of Taarab while remaining true to its historical depth and cultural roots.

Keeping Taarab Alive

Taarab is not just music – it is a living tradition, a cultural lexicon, and a poetic form of storytelling that has defined Zanzibar for centuries.

As a composer and performer, my mission is to ensure that this art continues to flourish – honoring the past while embracing the future.

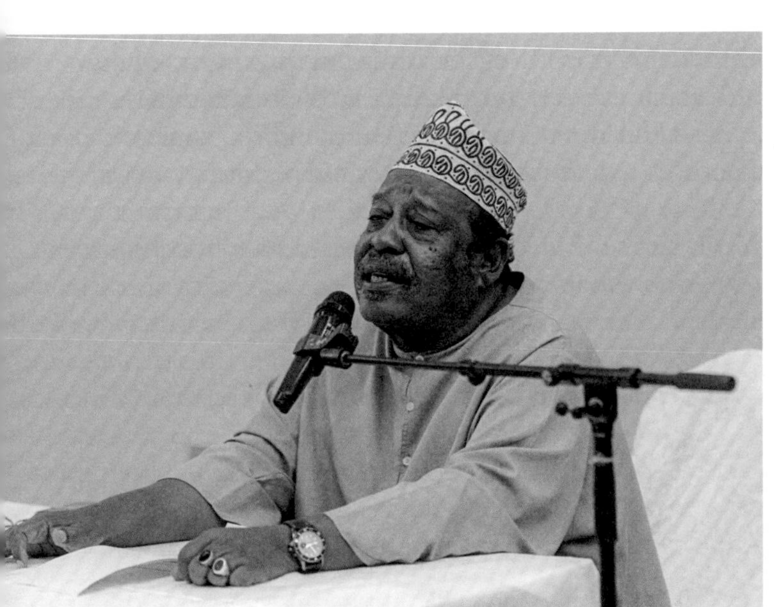

Simply Making Nature

conversation with Tanka Fonta

  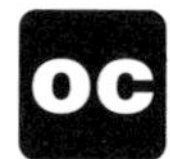 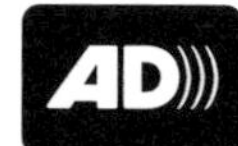

Text developed from a
conversation between the Fundação
Bienal team, Alya Sebti (co-curator
of the 36th Bienal) and the artist on
February 22, 2025.

Why Insects Fly?

On my first day of school, I think I was four and a half years old, and my mama's friend, who was my teacher, came to our house and took me by the hand. I was just a little guy and we had all these giant kola nut trees at the time. No electricity, but still a very beautiful and pristine area. The school was not too far from home, and that first encounter with the other kids wasn't in a class-room. Instead we played in the fields, chasing grasshoppers, and rolling around on the grass – just like the lush, carpet-like grass at Ibirapuera Park.

Around the age of seven, I joined a small school band. The older boys played side drums, and I became fascinated. I got so interested and began learning masquerade dances and started experimenting with crafts. We used to make bamboo cars with wire and invent all sorts of things. I believe a child's phil-osophical journey begins early – chil-dren are naturally curious. They want to know why the tree is green, why the grasshoppers have different colors, why they fly. Society often stifles this curiosity, and philosophy becomes something reserved for Western thinkers. But that's patently false. The etymological meaning of philosophy is "love of truth." It belongs to everyone. We're born with a philosophy. For me, it started very early.

I became interested in instru-ments because I was already immersed in sound – insects, animals, plants. Looking back, much of the music we make is simply nature. Every society has mastered sound and light, modulating them to express what we feel and think. We developed language and scripts to convey meaning – through music, painting, or other forms.

When I was thirteen, my mom gave me a book with an image of a spacecraft NASA had launched.[1] It showed a diagram representing humanity, created in a symbolic language meant for extraterrestrial beings. So, if there is any alien civi-lization and they pick up this diagram, they would know that there are human beings on place called Earth. That image lit a fire in my imagination. I couldn't fully grasp it at the time, but I started thinking about symbolic languages beyond written words. I think a lot of the seeds of the work I'm doing now may have come from that period.

My father's village had its own script – I think they call it the *Bamum scripts*.[2] I found out that my grandfather worked for a Sultan who created a unique ideographic writing system. Maybe subtle influ-ences came through genetically. There were no artists in my imme-diate family – just academics or

95

common people – but my grandfather was a scribe, like an archiver for the Sultan, at this place where my father comes from. I think that influenced me.

As children, we spent a lot of time in the rivers and bushlands, curious and always investigating. I developed a love for botany early on. When I read about plants or animals, I wanted to know what studying them was called. My older brother said, "That's botany. That's zoology." I was lucky to have many intellectuals in my family – my mom, my father, my uncles – and our house was filled with books. When I got curious, I read.

Where Do Sounds Come From?

By age fifteen, I had read all 24 volumes of *Funk & Wagnalls Standard Encyclopedia* we had at home. My mom, impressed, bought me Dante Alighieri's works. My imagination was ablaze. But when I went to school, there was no opportunity to study art. I excelled in science – geology, physics, chemistry – and chose botany. My heart was in art, but we had no money for art. I ended up spending more time playing guitar, being a rascal, than attending lectures.

After three years, I realized something profound: all subjects are interconnected. Geography, botany, music – they all share a common root. Maybe we just divide them to have administrative control, but at their core, they're about perception and naming. In my work, I connect them through what I call *vibrational languages*.

How did musicians centuries ago create sounds that NASA only recently recorded?[3] They had to amplify them fifty times and they sound exactly if you are playing a violin or a piano. I believe we carry ancient memories – remnants from the beginning of time. How else could musicians replicate cosmic sounds only modern instruments can capture? When a musician plays them today, audiences feel it viscerally. They don't need explanations.

Where Do Colors Come From?

I had never been to São Paulo, but I stood before a tree and thought, "I've seen this before." Call it madness, but artists or creative people express such phenomena through poetry or music. You don't need a form, nor a text, nor a telephone – just pure mind-to-mind exchange. Conventional education isn't equipped to explain this. That kind of communication comes from love. When you love someone, you understand them without speaking.

As I said before, our earliest mastery was of sound and light. Communication wasn't just verbal; it was chemical, sonic. Trees and animals still use these methods. Humans evolved language to express emotion and thought – things too complex for chemistry. But language can limit us. It's just one protocol among many.

Do Colors Have Sounds?

I wanted to find out why we invented instruments. So, I returned to my childhood. We made flutes from papaya stems, punching holes without ever seeing a factory-made flute. The vocal cords have limits, because they have a specific frequency range. So, if I have extended forms of thought which I develop and call instruments, I can get finer vibrations which I can use if I want to communicate things the words cannot. I need the violin, the cello or the drums, because they work in a higher frequency range.

But even written philosophical texts are limited – our vocabulary and languages are young. How do you describe phenomena with no name? Or dreams, or visions? Even if you combine Japanese, Portuguese, German, English, or all the languages in the world, you'd fall short. Artists step in where language ends. With colors, sounds, instruments, they reach beyond speech.

In early education, this is instinctively understood. We have to include art, music, we have to include various elements when teaching kids. And I think in this part of the world people already understood that, because in the kindergarten they teach them art, how to mix colors, how to play instruments – these help the students learn. Composing music is like writing an essay. One uses instruments, another uses words. Strip away the categories, and you'll see the essence: sharing something, telling a story.

Improvisation reveals this. Musicians play together without planning, anticipating one another. The mind is capable of this real-time coordination. The things that keep us from not being able to improvise in many areas is the resistance or fear. What is it that prevents a mind to be receptive? Find out what is the impediment that keeps you not able to improvise.

You need confidence. When you remove that impediment, we are vibrating in the same frequency. If I'm going away, you already know that. You will join me on the other route. You leave the mind open, because the mind has this capacity. It's how we form friendships too – by accepting each other's imperfections. Western systems often compartmentalize everything, limiting flexibility. But true improvisation comes from openness.

Even mistakes are part of the beauty. Many musicians make them, but audiences never notice. The process continues, finding harmony. Industrial systems, like Henry Ford's[4] assembly line, turned people into parts. Schools fragmented the mind. But ancient philosophers embraced all subjects – natural sciences, medicine, art.

If someone learns biology, they should also study color. Where do colors come from?

I Want to Be Happy, and I Am Here for That

Children excel in subjects like art and music because these expand the mind. Teaching color can help with chemistry. Many struggle with formulas, but different brains need different paths. I once had a physics teacher who saw we loved drawing and adapted the lessons. Suddenly, we loved physics. He showed us the frequency of colors, and it clicked.

That's alternative learning. It's unfair to praise only those who excel in calculations. Not everyone will be a doctor or astrophysicist. Everyone has something to offer. In school, we must break orthodoxy. Let kids sing and dance. They'll learn because movement and music release brain chemicals. Children do this naturally. As adults, we forget and turn to doctors. But Samba can do what medicine cannot.

Music and art bring joy. They open minds. Teach children with drums and rhythm, and they'll want to learn. See more at Prozac – just a little spice in the lesson.

I practice my instruments daily because if I stop, I won't be myself. I want to be happy. It's not trivial – it's essential. That's what the mind and body are for. And that is why I'm here.

1   The Pioneer Plates, created by scientist Carl Sagan, were sent into space on the Pioneer 10 and 11 probes in the 1970s. Containing symbolic representations of humanity and the location of the Earth, they were intended for possible extraterrestrial civilizations. See more at: https://science.nasa.gov/resource/pioneer-plaque/. Accessed in Feb. 2025.
2   The Bamum writing is a writing system developed for the Bamum language at the end of the 19th century by King Ibrahim Njoya. The pictographic, and later syllabic, writing was used until the beginning of the 20th century in what is now the territory of Cameroon. There are currently efforts to revitalize it as part of Cameroon's cultural heritage. See more at: https://eap.bl.uk/project/EAP051.
3   Since 2020, the "NASA sonification" project has sought to transform astronomical data into audible sounds. Using images captured by telescopes, NASA converts characteristics of celestial objects into sound frequencies, creating musical compositions that represent space phenomena. To see more: https://chandra.si.edu/sound/. Accessed in Feb. 2025.
4   Henry Ford (1863–1947) developed and popularized the so-called "production line," mass-producing automobiles. The production line is an organized manufacturing system in which a product is assembled or processed sequentially in several fragmented stages, with each station or work point dedicated to a specific task. In this way, each worker at each station is only responsible for a tiny part of the entire assembly, like hammering a nail.

A Female DJ in Zanzibar

Aisha Bakary (Hijab DJ)

Peace be upon you. My name is Aisha Bakary Mohammed. I was born in Zanzibar.

My mother is from Pemba, and my father was also born there. So, I am proud to be Zanzibarian. I was born in 1995, and I am a mother, a wife, and a musician – something that for many women is really. But in a woman's life, there are stages she must go through: a time for marriage, a time for motherhood.

I am grateful to be someone who believes in embracing all these stages. I won't speak for too long – I would rather give space for questions. I studied at Kidonge Chekundu from primary through secondary school. Then I enrolled at university to study IT, earning a diploma after two years, and later pursuing a degree in engineering. I left that path and turned to music. While studying, I also worked as a radio presenter, first at Radio Cairo Swahili for nearly two years. But it was all part of searching – trying to find myself. In the search for purpose, we try many things we believe might lead to success.

I worked at Clouds FM in Dar es Salaam, although I didn't like to be seen. That's why I chose radio instead of TV. I had offers for television, but my family is very religious and conservative. Appearing in public would have been difficult for them to accept.

I remember winning the Clouds Plus award one year for best presenter from Zanzibar. My friend Mr. Stika, the MC, really encouraged me to continue, but I had to step back due to my family's disapproval. Later, I moved into music – something I've always loved deeply.

I started in music around 2017–2018. Initially, I dreamed of becoming a producer, because I didn't want to be seen. People could come to the studio, work with me, and that was it. But again, my family did not support my choice. While in the studio with Marsh Marley – who has been instrumental in my career – he told me, "If you want to be a producer, you have to start as a DJ so you learn how to mix." That's when I began DJing, and I discovered I loved it even more than producing.

Seeing people enjoy the music I mixed made me feel alive. That's where my journey began. Why do I cover my face? It's because, when I started, I didn't want my family to know I was doing music. They would have crushed my dream early on. My mother is very strict and believes that a woman should focus on education, get married, and live quietly with her husband.

So I worked during the day only. I asked Marsh Marley to schedule me only for daytime work, because I had never been to a nightclub. I had never done a night event.

103 Eventually, though, I had to start working at night. Marsh told me,

"Daytime work won't last forever – you'll have to take night gigs." So I began covering my face to hide my identity. Sometimes I would return home at 3 or 4 am and find the doors locked. Being a young woman out that late was controversial. I faced many challenges.

One day, an aunt saw me performing at a wedding. She looked at me and said, "Aren't you Aisha?" I said yes, and she filmed me. When my mother asked, I had to tell her the truth: that I had been doing this for almost a year, and I begged her forgiveness, because it's what I love.

We quarreled. My father was especially hurt. He said, "I thought you were at university." I told him I had dropped out nearly a year earlier and was now pursuing music. That was the beginning of the Hijab DJ brand – born out of struggle.

I kept performing, though my family never fully accepted it. As Bi Rukia said yesterday, sometimes parents might understand, but society still applies pressure. People questioned my parents: "Why let your daughter go to clubs?"

But if you have a dream, you must pursue it with all your strength. In 2019, I received my first award in Zanzibar – from the Women's Foundation in Norway – as Woman of the Year. That same year, I received another local award. In 2020, I received an award from the Republic of Korea as Best Young Influencer. In 2022, I received another award in Zanzibar. In 2024, I was nominated by Clouds FM in mainland Tanzania as Woman of the Year. I've had the opportunity to perform abroad, including in Saudi Arabia, and to join a panel there.

I also worked in Dubai for eight months. It has been a long journey, full of challenges. As a woman, it's not easy. But I keep going. It's still early. We work hard to make things happen – so that others, especially girls coming after us, can learn from our paths.

Whatever I do, I know other women are watching and learning. I hope that one day – even 100 years from now – someone will come along, do something different, and say, "I was inspired by DJ Hijab."

You don't have to be a DJ. There are many things you can be. But I hope my story can be a source of inspiration.

So I welcome you. There's more to the story. I invite your questions and suggestions – but I won't accept any suggestion that I quit music. Welcome, everyone.

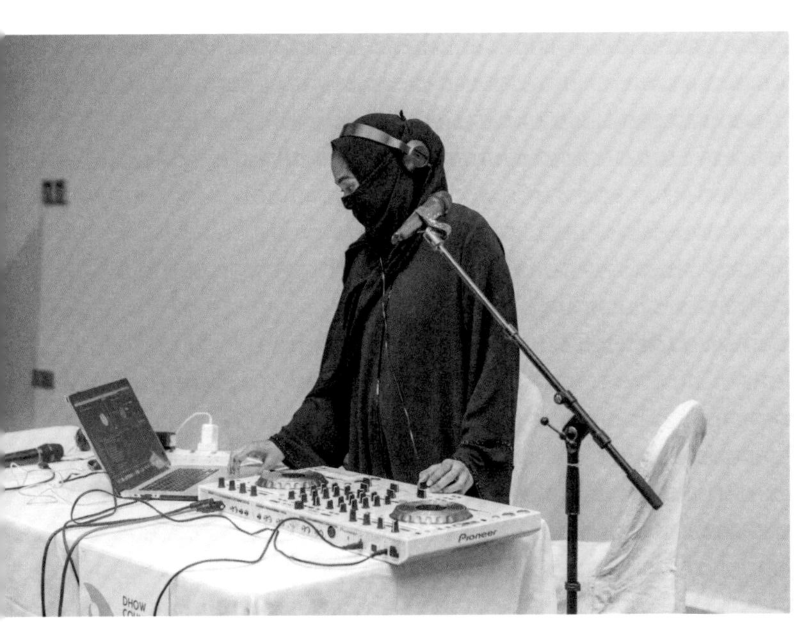

Taarab: An Audience Experience in the Heart of Zanzibar

Mohamed Ameir Muombwa

When discussing or writing about music, the focus often lies primarily on the music itself, its songs, or the musicians. The audience, however, is seldom highlighted unless specifically mentioned. Yet, I believe music is incomplete without its audience, as it is ultimately created for them. The importance of the audience in completing the musical experience has inspired me to share my personal perspective as an audience member during a Taarab performance in Zanzibar. What I will present today is a unique view, one that may differ from others' experiences at Taarab events. Nonetheless, like any art form, Taarab affects people deeply, each in their own way.

I was born and raised in Mzuri Kaja Makunduchi, a place entirely devoid of Taarab music. The sounds of my childhood were shaped by the traditional *ngomas* of Makunduchi, such as Mahumbwa and Msanja. In fact, I had never even heard of Taarab music until later in life. The closest sound I encountered that resembled Taarab was *Kidumbak* – often referred to as "little Taarab" –, perhaps because there was a *Kidumbak* group in my village.

Had my brother not chosen to marry a second wife, I might have remained unfamiliar with the intricate world of Taarab. His decision deeply saddened his first wife, who, in search of solace, began attending Taarab performances and asked me to accompany her. I believe the music brought her great comfort, and she continued to invite me along. Through these experiences, my own love for Taarab gradually grew. The more I attended, the more captivated I became. Eventually, I became an avid fan.

During Eid al-Fitr celebrations in Zanzibar, it is common for two Taarab orchestras – Malindi and Culture – to perform. My journey into the world of Taarab began after hearing radio announcements about performances by these two groups. These broadcasts presented an opportunity to plan a special evening out with my wife. Her enthusiastic "yes" would set off a series of events, including turning our bedroom into a romantic retreat. I could sense her excitement as she prepared, choosing her outfit and applying perfume. Sometimes, she would ask my opinion on her look, seeking my approval for her public appearance. As the time to leave approached, we would share a growing sense of anticipation.

Outside the venue, while waiting to buy tickets, I always noticed the warm, familial atmosphere surrounding these events. Every Taarab performance I've attended has been marked by exchanges with familiar faces in the crowd. We would greet one another, crack jokes, and fill the air with laughter. With my wife by my side, I was mindful to avoid any behavior that might spark jealousy, often engaging more with the male audience, as women usually outnumber men.

In the hall, I usually choose a seat in the back row to fully absorb the ambiance. My eyes sweep across the room, much like a camera, scanning for captivating sights. The stage's vibrant colors always catch my attention. While such color choices may not spark much discussion elsewhere, in Zanzibar, they often prompt commentary. This is due to Zanzibar's politically sensitive climate, once defined by rivalry between the Chama Cha Wananchi (CCW) and Chama Cha Mapinduzi (CCM) parties. A predominantly blue stage was associated with CCW, while green symbolized CCM.

Despite the political tension, Taarab has played a vital role in uniting Zanzibaris, even if only temporarily, under the shared umbrella of entertainment. Both major Taarab clubs, Malindi and Culture, continue to attract audiences across the political spectrum.

People attend Taarab performances for many reasons – cultural connection, social interaction, entertainment, emotional expression, or intellectual engagement. Personally, I go for entertainment, emotional expression, and intellectual stimulation as a journalist. I particularly enjoy watching women dance to the rhythm of Taarab instruments, their graceful hand movements. However, what I enjoy most is when my favorite songs are performed by the artists who made them famous. Among my favorites are "Muungwana" [The noble/respectable one], by Professor Mohamed Ilyas, "Kwenye Telefon" [On the telephone], by Rukia Ramadhani, and "Haya ni Maumbile Yangu" [This is my nature], by Fatma Issa. While I love many Taarab songs, I will focus on these three and explain how they resonate with me.

I'm drawn to "Muungwana" not just for its themes, but for the way it is performed. The rising and falling of the artist's voice is so captivating that when I'm feeling stressed, I find myself singing the line I love: "*Niiiimeshajenga ukuta, niiivugumu kuubomoa*" [I have already built a wall, it is hard to demolish]. I even used this line once to lighten a marital disagreement and it worked. I adapted it to say: "*Oooh mke wangu sina makosa, ooh hakika wanionea.*" [Oh, my wife, I have no faults; truly they are picking on me.]

Another song that has captured my heart is "Kwenye Telefon" by Rukia Ramadhani. The way she sings this song transports me, and I imagine myself as a child being gently rocked to sleep. The lyrics cleverly weave together the romantic phrases lovers exchange over the phone, transforming them into poetic music. One line especially resonates with me: "*leo unanikumbuka ni Fulani bila shaka*" [Today you remember me – surely it's so-and-so].

The third song, "Haya ni Maumbile Yangu" by Fatma Issa, holds a special place in my heart. I was present the first time she performed it live, and her emotional delivery left a lasting impression. It was the only Taarab song that ever moved me to tears. It felt as though Fatma was asserting her individuality, responding to those who had criticized

108

her. Knowing that many people say bad things about Fatma Issa, I empathized with her when she decided to respond through music.

When it comes to Taarab musicians who play instruments, my favorites are: Nassor Amour Abdallah, known as Cholo Ganun, who plays the qanun; Mohamed Issa Haji, known as Matona, who plays the violin; and Tryphon Evarist, who plays multiple instruments.

Cholo stands out for his total immersion while playing the qanun, doing it like no one else in Zanzibar. In my opinion, he is the master of the qanun. Matona's violin is equally impressive: his playing feels like multiple instruments at once. I always look forward to his performances.

Then there is Tryphon Evarist. Though short in stature, he stands tall in the world of Taarab. This talented young artist excels at nearly all Taarab instruments. I affectionately refer to him as Mr. Fixer, due to his multifaceted role in Taarab: teaching, singing, playing instruments, and writing musical notation. With his dedication and expertise, it is reassuring to know that when the current greats are gone, Taarab will remain in capable hands – his.

Taarab performances have evolved over time. Originally, Taarab was associated with sitting and listening, but it has become a more vibrant form that encourages dancing. Furthermore, Taarab has branched into two major styles: traditional and modern, with the latter being more suited to dance.

As a senior citizen, I prefer traditional Taarab. It feels like a wise teacher guiding his students through life's challenges, as traditional Taarab touches almost every aspect of human experience.

To sum up, Taarab has been a steadfast source of entertainment for Zanzibaris since its introduction by Sultan Sayyid Baragash bin Said in the 1880s. It has been a source of comfort and joy to its people During the era of Siti Binti Saad – considered the queen of Taarab –, her recordings in Bombay helped promote Zanzibar to the world. More strikingly still, she was the first female Taarab singer to record her songs. Taarab has taught life lessons through lyrics, serving as a cultural identity marker for Zanzibar, and entertaining visiting dignitaries. It promotes peace and unity, supports livelihoods, allows women to express marital grievances creatively. Without Taarab, Zanzibar would be like food without salt – technically edible, but flavorless. Let us preserve it for future generations.

The Making of a Taarab Musician

Tryphon Evarist

Good morning, peace be upon you, and welcome. My name is Tryphon Evarist, I'm a musician from Zanzibar. I'm also a teacher and an Artistic Director at the Dhow Countries Music Academy (DCMA). Today, I've prepared to talk about the impact and/or influence of DCMA on the traditional Taarab musical life of Tryphon Evarist. I'm personally going to be the witness of this. I'll talk about my life before and after joining DCMA.

But before that, I want to sincerely thank and honor Hijab DJ. Personally, it's always been my plea to see women doing things people think they can't. I didn't know her well before. But if I liked her work a little before, from this day on I fully admire her – for her experience and persistence, never giving up. She's a huge inspiration. Congratulations for proving that. I'm a fighter like her.

To prove that I'm a fighter like her, before proceeding, I'd like you to listen to some of my non-Taarab songs. Then we'll listen to what I've done in Taarab. This song is for young people who tend to think but don't take action by working. They just talk without acting. I love this song and so do a lot of people – it's called "Pambana," "fight." Let's listen briefly, then I'll play another track, so you know what Tryphon Evarist does [music]. This is "Pambana." "Wachana na maneno" means "stop talking, take action."

This next song is called "Sofia." Let's listen briefly. Those are some of my works. Later we'll see how DCMA helped me reach the point of composing traditional Taarab.

I'll show you some visuals from my early life. That's me as a chubby little kid with my cousins and children from the village where I grew up [shows some pictures]. I was born in Zanzibar in 1992, in Bega Moja. Later, my family moved to Kizimbani, where I was raised. I loved music from a very early age, even though I wasn't academically involved in it. I used to write random poems and lyrics. Some people still remember those childhood rhymes. When we meet, they remind me, and I just laugh them off as childish. Now I've grown and evolved. I was a hustler.

I used to do many things – truly many. I've always loved learning new things. Before DCMA, I worked in a hotel as a housekeeper. I was good with both electric and manual tools. I was also a barber – one of the best. Give me clippers and I'll handle it. A friend of mine refused to get his haircut by anyone else when I moved to town from Dole County. He also paid another barber for us to use his salon, so I could cut his hair. I also played football a lot. I'll show some pictures as proof. And I played baseball and was even a member of Zanzibar's national team. I was once the assistant coach of a baseball team here in Zanzibar.

I was also a farmer – I knew how to grow rice, cassava, leafy greens, and more. I even produced and sold charcoal. Give me tree trunks

111

and I can make you charcoal out of it. I sold *urojo* [Zanzibari soup] during Ramadan. I'd go to my cassava field and make chips for the *urojo* I'd sell. So, a few days before Ramadhan, I'd prepare myself financially for this business and get other items from a nearby market (namely Mwanakwerekwe). I'd cook everything myself – *kachori, badia, mishkaki,* you name it. Even the soup itself, I could make it in three different ways. I also worked as a spice tour guide. I went through all that before DCMA. You'll see photos as evidence – Tryphon as a footballer, baseball player, spice guide.

So, in life, giving up is not an option. I always say, for those of us with some faith – we now know why God dislikes those who give up. I used to wonder why, but now I know. Once you commit to something, it's not just about you anymore. People start looking up to you. If after a year of working on something, six people were inspired to follow you, and then you suddenly quit and move on to doing something else, what happens to these people who looked up to you? So, whatever you do, just never give up – because when you give up, you're ruining the lives of many who looked up to you. That's why even God hates it when people give up. If you have an idea, don't leave it in your mind – act on it the next day. All these things I did weren't easy, as I went through struggles too.

For instance, as a football player, I was often being benched. Sometimes the coach would say, "If you miss practice, you don't play." There were three other guys who played the same position as me. Two of them often skipped practice. But I'd show up. If others skipped practice, I knew I'd have a chance. Then, one day before the game, they'd show up, and the coach would choose them and leave me out – it hurt, but I never gave up. Eventually, I earned my spot in the starting eleven. Until I stopped playing football. Therefore, every field presents its own challenges, even baseball, anything I got involved in, it wasn't easy. This was my life before joining DCMA. Now let's see how I found out about DCMA. It's a long story, but I'll make it short.

I learned about DCMA when I was working as a housekeeper at a hotel. One day, after work, I went to my room and turned on the radio – something I rarely did. But that day I did – and I think it was divine intervention. I heard an ad from DCMA: "Wether you have talent or not, but is eager to learn music, there's a one-year scholarship." I jumped out of bed, reached for my notebook, and wrote down the audition date. Before then, I didn't know Zanzibar had a music school. I came to town, asked around, and found it – back then it was located at the Old Customs House near Mizingani.

At the audition, there were around seventy people. Unfortunately, most of them had experience with instruments or singing. I had none.

When I arrived, I was asked what I came for – I said, "Singing." I sang something. I don't know if the judges liked it, but I was put aside. Then they asked if I'd like to try an instrument. I said, "Piano" – because I'm Christian and had seen it in church. I was told to try it, but I didn't know how, so I just tapped randomly. Then they gave me drums – same thing. They handed me a qanun as well, but the same thing happened, as I had no experience.

I was moved again and again to try different instruments. I wasn't among the selected. They wanted fifty; we were more than that. Luckily, DCMA had something special – they decided to admit all of us. My teacher Thabit instructed someone: "Bring that boy an accordion." I was handed the instrument for the first time and asked to play. He asked me to put on the accordion, and I asked him, "And then what?" He told me to play the instrument. They showed me how: "Pull here, step there." And that's how it started… Even though I didn't like the accordion and had never considered learning it, I agreed, because one thing I know is that a teacher can see something bigger in you than what you can see in yourself. They must have seen something in me. So, I said, I will learn this instrument.

While I was attending DCMA, I was still working at a hotel. There was a small challenge regarding the day scheduled for music theory. And the teacher was Elder Thabit. His class was on Saturdays. And Saturday was a day I was supposed to be at work [the call to prayer is heard]. Okay, alright, five more minutes – just a little call of prayer, then we'll resume…[1]

Now, we continue. The theory class was on Saturdays, and Saturday was the day I was supposed to work. The students were doing their first semester exams. I was lucky enough to do the practical instrument exam, but I missed the theory exam. When I approached Mr. Thabit to request to do the theory exam, he refused. He told me, "Since you don't attend class, I won't allow you to sit for the music theory exam."

I thought deeply, because I didn't want to fall behind; I wanted to progress equally in both instrument and theory. If I was in Grade 1 for instrument, I wanted to be in Grade 1 for theory as well. Not one ahead of the other. So, I made a very tough decision. I said, "It's fine," and I quit my job, so that I could attend Thabit's theory class on Saturdays. I left my job at the hotel and decided to focus on music. I agreed to start over completely. Later, when I saw I was struggling a lot, I even quit working in a salon, I quit football, I quit baseball.

I started over because God has given me the ability to become whatever I want. But of all the things, music has taken the biggest space in my life. I mean, if I wanted to study law, I would succeed thanks to the talent God has given me – *Alhamdulillah*,[2] I don't take it for granted. But I said, "Music is what I love most." So, I agreed to let go of everything and start anew.

113

I was struggling. I couldn't even afford transport fare to go to DCMA, nor food. I would leave home early in the morning, stay at the school all day, and get back home in the evening. I developed ulcers from staying hungry. You see, nothing in life is easy. I got that wound. But I told myself, "Whatever happens, so be it."

A very important person in my music journey, who I must mention, is a certain woman – she's here today – this is Rukia [Ramadhani]. She has had a huge impact on my music journey. For those who don't know – whatever happens, I love and appreciate her deeply.

It happened like this. I remember I had no money for transport. I said to myself, "If I find my mother at home, I'll ask her for fare." Fortunately, I found my mom and asked her, "I'm going to school and I don't have the fare." She gave me 1,000 shillings. At that time, I was in Dole. The fare was 500 to go, 500 to return. I arrived late to class. When I got into the music theory class, everyone had already started.

Rukia asked me, "Why are you late today?" I said, "It's not just being late – I almost didn't come at all. Fare is a huge challenge for me." She said, "Let's talk after class." We talked, and she asked, "How much is your daily fare?" I told her, "1,000 shillings – 500 to go, 500 to return." She said, "From now on, I will give you 5,000 shillings every week, starting today." So, wherever I go, I mention her. I thank God for her. She played a major role in my success.

My mother didn't like me doing music. When I left my job at the hotel, I didn't tell my family. My father had already passed, but my mother was still alive. I used a clever excuse. I told my mom, "At the hotel, I spend too much time and my mind is still young – I need to learn more. Let me leave the hotel and focus on studying." I got her blessing with that story.

Later, when she found out, she came to DCMA and said, "Show me your teachers." She met them and they said, "This young man has talent – we'll take him under our wing." My mother said, "Please watch over him. He won't ask you for help even when he's in need." The teachers understood.

On graduation day, I received my certificate. I was the top student and got a 300,000 shillings award. But I was also doing things out of responsibility, unaware that people were noticing. In life, no matter your talent, without discipline, you have nothing. Discipline is crucial. I worked hard at school – not just learning instruments, but helping with different tasks. As a result, I was awarded "Best Student of the Year." I completed up to the diploma level. The woman in the picture is my mother. The others are my elder sister and aunt. You can also see Rukia there. I think Rahma [Machupa] graduated with me but I don't see her in the picture. There's nothing easy in life – I struggled a lot. But from all that, I eventually became a director. People saw my struggle and gave me a chance.

Let's talk about the strength of DCMA in Taarab Asilia, genuine, traditional Taarab. First, it encourages – it prioritizes traditional Taarab over other types of music. You'll hear Taarab playing everywhere on campus. Many trips for performances, both in and outside the country, are driven by Taarab Asilia. This encourages people to join. For those who dream of flying in planes, like me, Taarab was the path.

At DCMA, once students start getting good at playing instruments, there are two Taarab bands – one for beginners and one for advanced students. This shows how much DCMA is committed to preserving and promoting Taarab Asilia. Even during auditions, teachers guide students toward traditional instruments. They don't force, but they advise, saying, "This is our heritage." When it comes to scholarships, preference – up to 80% – is given to those learning instruments used in Taarab Asilia. So you can see how DCMA is deeply invested in preserving this tradition – by teaching, performing, even on digital platforms. We also preserve it through notation – written music lasts longer than other formats. DCMA also promotes Taarab through international travel – Poland, Abu Dhabi, Germany etc.

One of my own songs, "Nitakuoa," "I'll Marry You," is the first Taarab Asilia piece I composed, performed, and preserved in notation. It was composed and written by me. I learned to notate music at DCMA. Before that, I knew nothing about notation or Taarab Asilia. DCMA made me love and understand traditional Taarab. I learned about groups like Nadi Ikhwan Safaa and Professor Mohamed Ilyas. I read a book about their history – it celebrated 185 years in 2002 or 2005, I think. I was eager to join, and I'm now a proud member of Nadi Ikhwan Safaa. My role model in Taarab Asilia – in both composition and performance – is Professor Mohamed Ilyas. I always mention him in interviews. Another song I've preserved in notation is "Mapenzi ya Chacha" [Unreliable Love], from Nadi Ikhwan Safaa.

In 2023, I won the Amazon Foundation Music Award for Best Poet of the Year, with my poem "Kiwembe" [A razor]: "Kiwembe, I warn you, keep my secrets. / Even if they offer money, don't tell. / You've touched parts of my body – don't betray me." Second verse: "I leave with coins to find you where you are. / Your many hairs can be cut – it's your right. / I won't use a knife, I prefer your service. / You know me deeply." Third verse: "If you hurt me, I'll be exposed. / I pray you continue being blessed. / Keep my secrets – sugar sweetens tea like secrecy sweetens love." The music for this poem will be composed by my mentor, Professor Ilyas.

In 2004, at the Zanzibar International Music Awards, I won three awards: Best Male Vocalist, Best Traditional Instrumentalist, and Best Taarab Asilia Song of the Year. And finally, let's listen to my first Taarab Asilia song, "Nitakuoa" [music plays].

I can't do everything – but God can help me…

1   Prayer times in Zanzibar: Adhuhuri is in the afternoon from 12:30 pm to 1 pm, Alasir is from 3:35 pm to 4 pm, Maghrib is from 6:30 pm to 6:50 pm, and Ishaa is from 7:45 pm to 8:15 pm.

2   Praise Be to Allah / Praise Be to God.

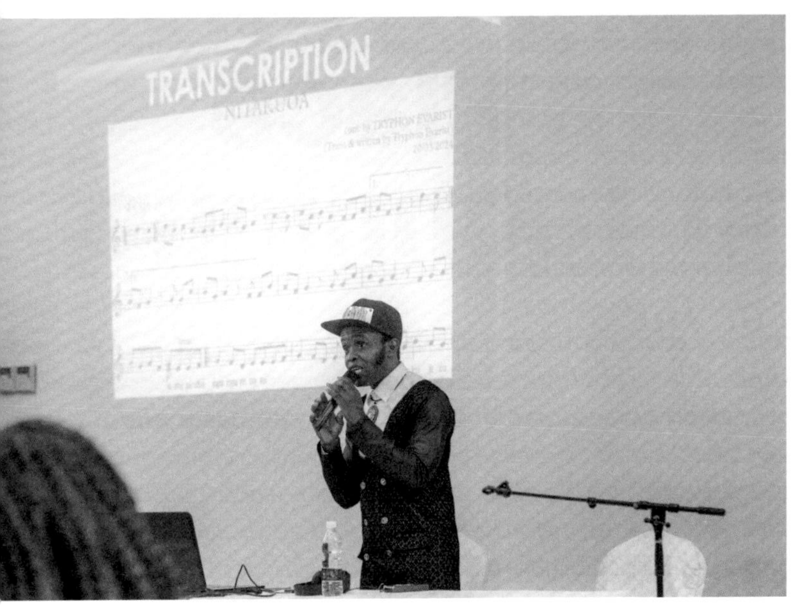

TRANSCRIPTION
NTJARUDA

Experiment, with *Fundamento*[1]

On Improvisation as a Place and Technique

Allan da Rosa

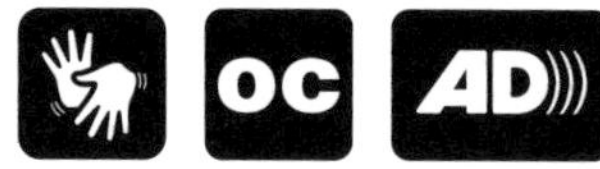

This text emanates from an *Angoleiro* inclination and breath. It is written by hands that were just playing the berimbau and pressing against the ground, that were held by mother and child, that wiped away the beads of sweat running down the neck, soaking the capoeira shirt. It is an apprentice's scripture lived within the vastness and flow of *capoeiragem* – this embodied, abstract, inflamed, serene, historical, practiced, and daily revered philosophical system, like bread kneaded by baking hands.

From the *Angoleiro* eyes, intimate with the ground, yet no more important than the *Angoleiro* ears, or the touching, stepping, and spinning, or the panting breathing, comes the sly pause, and the silver-tongued melodies the mouth sings as a choir. This is the conch from which I write this text, still warmly remembering the *roda de Capoeira Angola*[2] from hours ago. The *roda* reaches back centuries. And, as a ritual held every Friday night at the Senzalinha, in Taboão da Serra, with the Capoeira Angola Group Irmãos Guerreiros, led by Mestre Marrom (*IÊ, Viva meu Mestre!*),[3] it creates its own temporal dimensions in the *roda* itself, as well as in the cycle of reuniting every seven nights to form a continuous practice, intertwining with the many other social calendars that dictate our paths and interactions.

Roda: a full symbol of wholeness. Improvisation: a space shaped not only by spontaneity but also through trained technique, the kind that knows both the foundations and the gaps, the rules of the game, the kind that understands that the berimbau's wooden bows, the *vergas*, are the wood of an instrument, not a snooker cue, a golf club, or a baseball bat. Improvisation: spontaneity fused with study, that which adapts with magic to the surprises and rhythms of its surroundings, to a choreography woven within the heart of the unexpected.

Fundamentos that shape both technique and enchantment. One: knowing that the game begins with a blessing at the berimbaus' feet and is played in pairs. Two: having learned the teachings through call and response – in the chants, the rhythm of the instruments, the dance – we experience both playfulness and the unease when someone enters the *roda* still unaware of these fundamental pillars, but still plays, while exchanging knowledge brought from other houses, engaging with our language, weaving in new accents and grammars into our *floreio* [flourish]. That which unfolds in the sharp dangers and soft tenderness of each game with another body guided by rhythm, through the sung poem full of riddles, loopholes, and cunning. *"Bem-te-vi botou gameleira no chão,"*[4] uttered and sung in melismas, elongated syllables oscillating in pitch, hypnotizing, provoking. *"Pau rolou, caiu, no meio da mata, ninguém viu."*[5] But what might this encrypted message, this image, be, and why sing it now instead of another chant? *"O facão bateu embaixo, a bananeira caiu."*[6] Trees, as fruitful as the choirs that support the dance.

Technique: that which sprouts from commitment – in study, in training, in the ritual of practice that nurtures and deepens intimacy with language. It is a pursuit paved with discipline toward mastery of the instrument – mastery whose goal is not to diminish or constrain it, but to explore its depths, to make it bloom and honor it as a cocoon. Technique: a vegetable garden offered by every artist and every craftsperson to their art and culture, while nurturing and working with ancestral material. An offering to a community, composed of living beings, ancestral spirits resonating through the legacies they left behind, and those yet to come – who still have not arrived, yet are already here. Technique that demands dedication, whose fruits can inspire joy, rage, humiliation, solidarity, quiet mysteries, and astonishment. Technique, found in the gesture that repeats itself to reinvent and convey style with grit and grace. Technique for both affirming and challenging, broadly and specifically, what it means to be people. Technique, as moist as moldable clay, as moist as the saliva that kisses and utters secrets and satires and the saliva kept in the mouth, bathing silence. Technique, the very road between the gust of an idea and the concreteness of any finished work. Technique, the sea and the bridge between abstraction and matter, if the imaginary is that border between perfume and pores, between desire and its delightful fulfillment. Technique, for continuing the path and for changing the course, the step of reinventing the map. Technique, flavorful and committed, loving in its lightness, its rips, its sublime conduction, and in what it envelops and fascinates as communication.

Improvising with *fundamento*. Consider that what serves as a pillar, firm yet malleable, like the dialogue between a trio of berimbaus, was once an experiment that became a moving force. A cultivation rooted in the ancient ground of African sonic and communal technologies that shaped sounds known as bass, treble, and midrange (and we know that drum trios with the same arrangement and function are widespread in countless Black musical manifestations in *terreiros*, backyards, garages, stairways, street corners, and stages). Three berimbaus: *Gunga, Médio,* and *Viola.*[7] Three basic rhythms: *Angola, São Bento Pequeno,* and *São Bento Grande,* until the *Viola* rattles its sharp cries and laments – that is, if this is the *fundamento* of the house, since there are lineages that grant the *Gunga* the role of lead and bass soloist. Three tuned *urucungos* matching each other, composing the atmosphere, roundly resonating. Swinging and tear-inducing *urucungos,* conducting solemn and playful ambiances. To achieve this, one studies the weight, the angles, and the cadences in the process of learning how to hold the instrument, bringing it close or away from one's stomach, pressing or grazing the *dobrão* [a stone or a coin] against the *arame* [steel string], making it ring, listening to the orchestra it enmeshes in, and feeling the game between two bodies in the sly and highly perilous dance of kicks, head strikes, feints, simulations, and *gingas*. One must sit to learn: on the ground to listen, on the bench to play and build intimacy with the instrument. One must walk and move to learn, researching other havens and houses, other ways of making and ingenuities. Until, laughing or mourning, one proposes improvisation. *"Chora, Viola!"*[8] Until one experiments with *fundamento*, playing by the rhythm's rule, establishing sensitivities that translate and decipher our Being, full of loves, frustrations, contradictions, and dreams. Until one improvises, opening spaces and creating places that weave into ancestral times, generating forms and languages out of that which perhaps only poetic vibration can encompass, embedded in the most ordinary everyday life, in the most over-whelming dreams, in habits and routines, and in the flavors of living. Singing about cowherds, train tracks, rafts, markets, lovers' farewells, bravery, madness, ingratitude, a childhood that has passed but remains alive in the *Angoleiro* ways of *vadiar*.[9]

Improvisation and ground, water and air, rice and beans. Perhaps the very musculature of improvisation radiates, stretches, moves, contracts, expands, and expresses itself because of the ancient orthopedics of its ground. But who is sustaining whom?

If Capoeira Angola is an embodied philosophical system, it is sweaty theory, sophistication, and ingenuity of details; it is a web whose tiny parts are connected to every other millimeter; it is constellation and firefly, drop and ocean. And it is a haven of metaphors for everything that is pulsating, doubtful, painful, festive, and striking in life. And if it is something that is taught, then it communicates with every sort of pedagogy of living. Let us not forget the lines written by Mestre Pastinha (written… but why write if it was through absolute orality that he drew his philosophy?): *"Capoeira, Angola, Mãe. Mandinga de escravo em ânsia de liberdade, seu princípio não tem método e seu fim é inconcebível ao mais sábio capoeirista."*[10]

The African Caxambu chant from Minas Gerais weaves its call: *"Quem nunca viu, venha ver, caldeirão sem fundo ferver."*[11] A broad *fundamento*, a bleeding sacred enchantment, a tear-inducing imaginary brimming with bliss amid bruises, devoted to all that is enigmatic. In these ancient ways, whispering through our nights is the struggle with incompleteness, a dance with the fertile gap, made possible precisely by the cohesion of the system that opens itself to the feints in the game. Black Brazilian thought is a meticulously engineered system, balanced between rooted stability and the precarious edge of tricky situations, in the call to improvisation, where risk is a call to movement. And to improvise – to set a new moon in this sky – one must first respect the map of mysteries, the

121

fundamentos of this sovereign board, assembled and maintained amidst the vampiric history of a country built on the torture and bloodshed of Black people who, to this day, are killed simply for existing, for moving. These are the same peoples who organized nobilities, refined engineering, and shaped cultures both revered and stereotyped. Mystical techniques that have fascinated the entire world, yet here, in Brazil, have been scorned, ridiculed, and either confined to the spotlight of caricature or the terror of prison cells. They contend with the ignorance of those who, when visiting the *rodas*, sing and improvise without understanding the *fundamento* of the very verses they are uttering.

"*Todo o tempo não é um,*"[12] as we sing in the capoeira chant Siri de Mangue. Could there be a more elevated – or smaller and subtler – philosophical web of temporal dimensions than the one germinated within these gourds? Culture is also a web of rhythms, the wile of cadences, the wisdom of sensibility, the fascination of languages that enter and fertilize the blend of courage and fear in the dance with life. A dense and flowing web of forms and expressions born out of both necessity and joy. To bring people together, to simply be (oneself), to be people – not severed nor isolated in the so-called frozen or boiling individual, the social being, a number, statistics. People, challenging with their presence, as etymology suggests. People, weaving between the labyrinths of their mind and the horizons of their own times, tastes, and tones, their coexistence with people, environments, and beings.

Eternal and unique, Naná Vasconcelos, the Pelé of percussion, despite the support of immeasurable research and experience, feared the censorship of *mestres* due to his inventiveness with the berimbau. Yes, culture can be painful and fearful, caught between preservation and innovation. Naná Vasconcelos – a Mestre as well – built a garden on this border, and altered the instrument's physiology, from the berimbau's making to the ways of experiencing each of its parts, creating out of necessity and pleasure while searching for his own sonority, his own way of holding the *verga*, new angles for positioning the *dobrão*, for striking the *arame*, for shaking the *caxixi*, highlighting each part. Composing enchantment, inventing fruit on the ancient tree, boldly experimenting with the firm *fundamento* of spreading *mandinga*.

122

1   Fundamento [foundation, ground, bedrock], in Brazilian Portuguese. In this text, the author is employing a specific African-Brazilian usage of the word, related to African-Brazilian religious and cultural contexts. It can be read as principle, secret, ritual. [All the footnotes here are translator's notes.]

2   Capoeira Angola circle.

3   "IÊ, Long Live My Master!"

4   "The great kiskadee knocked the gameleira tree to the ground."

5   "The log rolled, it fell, hidden from sight, deep in the dell."

6   "The machete struck low, [and] the banana tree fell."

7   The three main types of berimbau used in capoeira.

8   Cry, *Viola*!

9   Wandering, loitering. In capoeira practice, it means being playful in your moves.

10   "Capoeira, Angola, Mother. *Mandinga* [sourcery, spell] of a slave yearning for freedom, its principle has no method, and its end is inconceivable to the wisest capoeira practitioner."

11   "If you haven't seen, come see it, a bottomless cauldron's boiling heat."

12   "All time is not one."

Educational Activities

The practices in the educational publication for the 36th Bienal de São Paulo are developed by the Fundação Bienal de São Paulo with the aim of bringing the world of contemporary art closer to different pedagogical contexts, promoting a type of education that recognizes subjectivity and the plurality of experiences, understanding those who take part as protagonists in these processes. It was built with teachers from São Paulo's public school system[1] and is in line with the Brazilian National Common Core Curriculum (BNCC) guidelines.

Designed as scripts for Creative Laboratories, these practices are structured into three meetings that can be adapted and incorporated according to the needs and possibilities of each context. They aim to encourage the construction of integrated knowledge and the expression of ideas, feelings, and reflections on social and cultural issues. In this case, the sequence of meetings takes creative processes with improvisational procedures as its point of departure. "Improvisation: Composing and Soundtracking Stories" proposes activities for the creation and sonic illustration of stories, while "Improvisation: Storytelling with the Territory" encourages reflection on material culture and the creation of stories in dialogue with the contexts in which the practices are carried out.

Improvisation: Composing and Soundtracking Stories

This series of meetings[2] includes activities for composing and soundtracking stories, using creative processes based on improvisation, in dialogue with material contained in this educational publication.

OBJECTIVES:

→ Relate contemporary art to everyday life;
→ Experiment with improvisation, composition and the soundtracking of stories;
→ Express musical ideas individually, collectively, and collaboratively;
→ Exploring different sources of sound, such as those from our own bodies (clapping, voice, body percussion).

NECESSARY SUPPLIES:

→ Computer, multimedia projector and speaker;
→ Bond paper or similar;
→ Writing materials (graphite pencils, felt-tip pens);
→ Materials that can produce sound (everyday objects);
→ Musical instruments.

DEVELOPMENT:

Improvisation appears across multiple artistic forms, such as theater, poetry, dance, music, and graffiti. There are countless ways to exercise creativity through improvisation, two of which are preparation and prior study. In this practice, we will explore improvisation with the creation and soundtracking of stories, engaging with the work of Naná Vasconcelos,[3] word games, and sound resources.

MEETING 1 – NANÁ

In this meeting, invite the participants to familiarise themselves with a soundtrack by Naná Vasconcelos. After interacting with the piece, hold a discussion to share interpretations and reflections on the different ways of telling stories through music, exploring the use of musical instruments and the sound of one's own body.

First, arrange participants in a circle. Then suggest listening to the song "Amazonas" by Naná Vasconcelos, from his 1973 album of the same name. The track can be found on streaming platforms or accessed via the QR Code.

After listening to the song, talk about it as a group. Here are some suggested questions for the conversation:

What instruments were used to compose this music?
What scenes does the artist represent through the sounds?
What stories does the artist tell through the sounds?

Encourage the group to create interpretations that go beyond the field of sound. If possible, during the discussions, invite participants to write down words or draw shapes that reflect their impressions of the music.

MEETING 2 – COMPOSING STORIES

In the second meeting, the group is invited to compose a story through improvisation, using words taken from the introductory text of *Invocation #3*, which took place in Zanzibar.

First, arrange the class in a circle and show them the collection of words. Discuss the possible meanings of each word:

COLLECTION OF WORDS:

- → HUMANITY
- → FEELING
- → RESILIENCE
- → CULTURES
- → MIXING

Invite the group to create a story, in the following way:

- → A participant draws or selects a word from the collection presented and begins a story inspired by it.
- → The story may begin with "Once upon a time."
- → The next participant continues the story, moving in a circular way.
- → Each person contributes a new passage, using improvisation as a creative tool.
- → The facilitator may introduce new words in the collection and thus shift the narrative direction.
- → The story must be recorded, either via audio, using a device such as a cell phone, or by a designated note-taker.
- → The decision to end the story should be made collectively.
- → Afterward, hold a group discussion about the experience.

Keep a record of the collectively created story and invite the group to bring instruments and sound objects to the next meeting.

MEETING 3 – SOUNDTRACKING STORIES

At this stage, invite the participants to soundtrack the story created at the previous meeting by experimenting with improvisations using different sound sources, such as their own bodies (clapping, voice, body percussion).

First, revisit the story from the previous meeting and talk about the possibilities of making soundtracks for them. Here are some suggested questions to get the conversation going:

> *What sounds can accompany the story?*
> *How to compose the sounds of the story?*

Invite the group to create a soundtrack to the story, as follows:

→ **The group is set up with instruments and sound objects;**
→ **Body percussion can also be part of the sound composition;**
→ **One person will be the reader or narrator of the story created;**
→ **Simultaneously, each person participates in making sound, experimenting with improvisations using different sound sources;**
→ **It is important that the soundtrack of the story is recorded using a recording device or by a person chosen to take notes;**
→ **The moment to end the story's soundtrack can be decided collectively;**
→ **When you have finished soundtracking the story, talk about the experience.**

Suggested questions for the conversation:

> *What was it like soundtracking the story we created?*
> *What were the discoveries and difficulties?*
> *What was it like to experiment with sound improvisation?*

Invite the group to research improvisation. One source of research could be the contents of this publication, such as the pieces by Ajíṭẹnà Marco Scarassatti and Allan da Rosa.

SUGGESTIONS FOR FURTHER WORK:

Based on the stories created and soundtracked by the class, draw up scripts for the production of video clips, animations, theatrical performances, etc.

Improvisation: Storytelling with the Territory

In this lab, we investigate material culture in a critical and creative way, as well as analyzing how the objects that surround us can shape our individual and collective experiences. Through observation exercises and improvised narratives, we will rethink the meaning of the elements around us and create stories from them.[4]

OBJECTIVES:

→ Relate contemporary art and everyday life;
→ Experiment with improvisation and the territory;
→ Represent places of experience;
→ Analyze and value cultural and material heritage.

NECESSARY SUPPLIES:

→ Bond paper or similar;
→ Writing materials (graphite pencils, felt-tip pens).

DEVELOPMENT:

In the various human cultures spread throughout the world, objects have social, aesthetic, and emotional value. They sometimes take on a sacred character, or become the guardians of the memory of events and people. It is common, for example, to call objects bought on trips or as gifts souvenirs. This reveals the ability of objects to go beyond their practical function and conjure feelings and memories.

Material culture is the set of objects and artifacts created by humanity throughout history. These objects not only reflect the practical needs of societies, but also carry symbolic and aesthetic meanings that help define the cultural identity of communities and individuals. Material culture can range from everyday utensils to works of art, and its analysis is fundamental for understanding how societies express themselves and differentiate themselves from one another.

MEETING 1 – MATERIAL CULTURE IN THE TERRITORY

The first stage of the lab involves an initial discussion about objects found in the area where the practice takes place. To this end, the mediator asks each participant to list at least five objects that he or she has noticed on the way from their homes to the practice site.

The lists can be requested in advance or can be made at the beginning of the meeting, after a moment of drift with the group around the place of practice.

When explaining the items on the list, it is essential to emphasize the importance of the adjectives of the objects found, so that none of them appear in an unspecified way.

EXAMPLES:

→ a perforated awning;
→ an old car;
→ an abandoned chair;
→ a garbage can made of tires;
→ a rusty cage.

Once the lists are completed, the mediator can organize a round for each participant to read theirs, without giving details about the objects or places where they were found. The group can then

131

reflect on the incidence of the same object in several lists, or the presence of a specific object in one of them.

This discussion should be accompanied by a consideration of the territory in order to get to know its features. Questions such as: What does this part of the city produce? What does this part of the city consume? How can this be understood from the objects we find on the street?

The mediator can ask the group what meanings the objects listed evoke for them. What does it mean to find these objects and how can we re-signify the territory from the things we find? What stories are told and what others can be imagined from what we find?

As the conversation draws to a close, we recommend collecting the lists to be used in the next stage of the lab.

MEETING 2 – MATERIAL CULTURE AND THE CREATION OF NARRATIVES

In the second stage, the mediator starts off by randomly redistributing the lists from the previous meeting so that each participant gets a different list. From then on, each participant will have time to articulate the items on the list in a short fictional narrative about their journey to the meeting.

Example (based on the list from Meeting 1):

*It started raining as I left the house, so I looked for shelter in vain, as all I found was a **punctured awning**. As if that wasn't enough, an **old car** drove through a puddle of water, splashing me. I was very upset; all I could do was sit on an **abandoned chair** next to a **garbage can** made of tires. That's when a huge rat appeared and tried to get into a **rusty cage** that had been left there.*

Once ready, the stories can be presented to the group. After the round of presentations, we recommend a discussion about the stories. The mediator can encourage analysis of the narratives, taking into account how elements of material culture feature in them. Do they only help to set the scene for the narratives created or do they bring some symbolism to what is being told?

In the example above, the objects on the list helped to create the scene of a degraded environment for the narrative of a person in difficulty on a rainy day. In this way, the mediator can encourage the group to analyze the content of their narratives and the setting in which they take place with the objects listed.

132

For this purpose, we recommend revisiting aspects of the conversation from the previous meeting, which sought to relate material culture to the territory in which the laboratory takes place.

Finally, the mediator can ask the group to re-read their stories and alter elements of the narratives, imprinting their impressions of the conversations and their experience in the territory on the objects listed.

At the end of the meeting, we recommend that the mediator collect the group's work for use in the next stage.

MEETING 3 – COLLECTIVIZING NARRATIVES

In the third stage, the mediator begins the activity by subdividing the group into groups of three, four or five, depending on the number of participants. The work from Meeting 2 will be distributed randomly, and each sub-group will have time to put the stories together to form a collective narrative.

The mediator can define a theme for the collective narratives or mobilize issues that are of interest to the territory and the community, based on what has emerged in previous meetings, as well as combining the process of writing the collective story with other available content.

The combined narratives can be used to compose characters, and the set of objects can be freely articulated to create environments in which, and with which, they interact. The subgroups are free to complement the narratives and alter the original content as long as they keep the objects listed.

At the end of the process, it is recommended that the groups present their narratives and talk about the relationship between the content of the narratives and the material culture of the territory.

SUGGESTIONS FOR FURTHER WORK:

From the results of the combination of narratives, scripts can be produced for animations, dramatizations, literature and cinema.

133

1   We would like to thank Bel Borges, Durval Mantovaninni, Gustavo Viana, Kaya Fernanda Vallim Braga Martins, Maria da Conceição Ferreira da Silva, Pamela Regina, and Rodrigo Pignatari for the rich exchanges that took place on October 26 and November 9, 2024.

2   This practice was developed in dialogue with BNCC skills: Elementary School – Early Years: Art: (EF15AR15); (EF15AR17); (EF15AR21). Elementary School – Final Years: Art: (EF69AR23).

3   Naná Vasconcelos, the stage name of Juvenal de Holanda Vasconcelos, born in Recife, Pernambuco, in 1944 and died in 2016 in the same city, was a renowned Brazilian percussionist, multi-instrumentalist and composer, recognized as one of the world's greatest percussionists. His main instrument was the berimbau, traditionally used in capoeira circles. Naná received numerous awards throughout his career, as well as making socio-educational projects possible, leaving an important legacy for Brazilian music.

4   This practice was developed in dialog with BNCC skills: Elementary School – Early Years: Geography (EF02GE08); (EF01GE09). Elementary School – Final Years: Art: (EF69AR31); (EF69AR34). Portuguese Language: (EF67LP23).

History of Taarab in Zanzibar and Worldwide

Bi Mariam Hamdani

Introduction

Taarab is a traditional music genre with a long history spanning over 130 years, continuing to be an important part of the cultural heritage of East African people, particularly in Zanzibar, Pemba, Mombasa, as well as in the Comoros Islands and some Arab countries.

Taarab music has traveled the world and gained international recognition. Taarab groups from East Africa have performed in various countries in Europe, the United States, and Asia, including China, Japan, India, and Arab countries like Oman, Kuwait, Dubai, Abu Dhabi, and Egypt, where Taarab has been performed multiple times.

Taarab has become a part of social life and entertainment, performed at weddings, family
celebrations, development events, political festivals, and even
social gatherings.

The spread of Taarab cannot be separated from the history of the Indian Ocean trade. During the monsoon seasons, traders from Arab countries, India, and other parts of the world would arrive in East Africa with various goods such as clothing, perfumes, incense, and other tools. But they also brought their cultures – clothing like the kanzu, *majokho*, *tarbush*, and *mabaibui* – as well as popular foods like biryani, pilau, *halua*, *bokoboko*, *sambusa*, *bhaji*, and chapati.

In addition to these, they also brought their arts and entertainment – rhythms from traditional dances like *sunsumia*, *razha*, *danedane*, and musical instruments like *tabla, oud, qanun* [Arabic zither], and *unasi* – elements that greatly contributed to the creation and development of Taarab music as we know it today.

The Origin of Taarab

The word Taarab comes from Arabic, meaning joy, entertainment, or excitement. Taarab music is a unique form of entertainment closely tied to the lives of the Swahili people, expressing emotions, love, teachings, advice, and life stories through lyrics and various musical instruments.

Taarab is a fusion of different cultures, where the sounds of instruments like the violin, guitar, qanun, oud, and violin are combined with songs that have influences from various languages and cultures, such as Arabic, Swahili, Hindi, and African. This music stirs emotions in the hearts of listeners and continues to be a way to communicate messages of social issues, love, teachings, and entertainment to the East African community and beyond.

137

The Introduction of Taarab in Zanzibar

The history of Taarab in Zanzibar officially begins during the reign of Sultan Barghash bin Said (1870–1888), although the roots of this culture go back to more distant commercial and cultural influences, notably through the monsoon trade (wind-driven trade).

The first royal descendant from Oman, Seyyid Said (1804–1856), moved his headquarters to Zanzibar in 1832. Despite his efforts to strengthen the island's economy through the clove trade and other goods, he was not fond of music. Likewise, his successor, Seyyid Majid (1856–1870), had no interest in music.

Major changes came with the reign of Barghash bin Said, who had the opportunity to travel to India during his exile after his failed coup attempt in 1859. While in India, Barghash became fascinated by developments in education, infrastructure, economy, and the arts – including music.

Upon returning to Zanzibar and assuming the throne in 1870, Barghash decided to promote Taarab music. He sent Mohamed Ibrahim (popularly known as Bai) to Cairo, Egypt, to study music, especially the playing of instruments like the qanun, oud, nay, and other Arabic instruments.

When Mohamed Bai returned to Zanzibar, he was tasked with establishing a Taarab music group within the Beit el Ajaib (House of Wonders), which he built in 1883. Instruments like the violin and other instruments were brought from Egypt, and Bai taught young Zanzibari people for a year and a half.

After the training was completed, a special Taarab performance was organized within Beit el Ajaib, which amazed both locals and visitors. From that point on, Taarab music began to be performed regularly, especially after dinner at the palace.

The Spread of Taarab Beyond the Palace

After the death of Sultan Barghash, his successors – Seyyid Khalifa (1888–1890), Seyyid Ali (1890–1893), and Seyyid Hamed (1893–1896) – did not show much enthusiasm for Taarab music. This situation allowed the common people to learn and develop Taarab outside the palace, particularly the youth from neighborhoods like Malindi, Mbuyuni, Kokoni, Vikokotoni, Kikwajuni, and Gongoni.

King Humud Bin Mohammed (1896–1902)

King Humud was fond of music and wanted Mohamed Bai to continue teaching both palace and street youths. He ordered more musical instruments to be imported from Egypt and strengthened the palace's Taarab group. This marked the beginning of the spread of Taarab among the general public of Zanzibar.

Taarab Beyond the Palace

When his son, Sultan Ali bin Hamud, inherited the throne, he continued to support music. He strengthened the Brass Band and the MaGoa band, while Taarab music continued to be played in the palace, and many talented young people had the opportunity to join.

These steps laid the foundation for the spread of Taarab in Zanzibar and eventually in East Africa. It became an important form of entertainment at weddings, celebrations, and various festivals – a musical heritage blending Arabic, African, Indian, and European influences.

Kidumbaki

Kidumbaki is a type of traditional music from Zanzibar with a long and unique history within the Swahili culture. This music began in the early 20th century and was associated with the common people, especially in urban areas like Ng'ambo. Kidumbaki uses simple instruments like violins, bass boxes, small drums, maracas, and *mkwasa*. The songs of Kidumbaki often accompany lyrics about daily life, love, satire, and social teachings. Kidumbaki also became an essential part of entertainment during weddings, social gatherings, and street celebrations, and continues to be an important aspect of Zanzibar's musical identity to this day.

The Formation of Taarab Groups[1]

In the second half of 1905, nine young men met and formed a club called Nadi Ibnaau l-Wattani Li-Jumuiat Ikhwan Safaa. These were: Abdallah Saleh Buaisha, Mohamed Ali Elyas, Abdalla Ambar Aboud, Said Ambar Aboud, Omar Abeid Al Haj, Mohamed Hilal Barwani, Sharif Salim Al Bedh, Mohamed Abeid Al Umar and Juma Kapen Bayashut.

They met at the home of Sheikh Naaman Mohammed Suleiman, and together they elected him as the honorary president (Rais Sharaf) of the club.

By December of that year, more young men had joined, bringing the total number of founding members to 17. It was then agreed to shorten the name to Nadi Ikhwan Safaa. This name was given by the Chief Kadhi (Islamic judge) of that time, Sheikh Ahmed bin Abubakar bin Sumeit.

Early Days of the Club

When the club was first established, it did not perform music. Instead, people would gather to play board games like bao, cards, and *dhumna* (a local game). The club was exclusively for men.

Two years later, the club ordered musical instruments, and after learning how to play them, they began performing songs – mainly Egyptian Arabic songs.

Women's Group

Around the same time, a women's group was formed called Nadi Ikhwati Safaa, but it did not last long.

There was also a group called Glasi Ngomeni from Malindi, which later merged with Nadi Ikhwan Safaa (nis). Another group called Anis l-Jalis was formed by dock workers (*makuli*), and this group became a serious rival to NIS, creating vibrant competition.

Emergence of Rival Groups

Nadi Ikhwan Safaa faced even greater competition when Nadi Shuubi was formed in Shangani. The songs performed and contested during this time were mostly Egyptian Arabic songs.

It wasn't until 1954 that NIS began composing songs in Swahili – one of their famous early Swahili songs being "Nyota Vingaravyo Wache Waseme" [The Shinest Stars Speak].

Siti Binti Saad (1920–1950)

She is regarded as the Mother of Taarab because of her immense contribution, especially in pioneering Taarab songs in the Swahili language. She was also among the first female artists in East Africa and was one of the earliest to record music in India with His Master's Voice.

Her songs became famous from East Africa all the way to Egypt. Siti was not only an artist but also like a social commentator – translating social and community stories into song. Examples of her songs include "Kijiti," "Kahamia Kianga Mselemu," "Fatuma Mzazi," "Paka Shume" [Stray Cat], "Kigalawa," "Muhogo wa Jang'ombe" [Cassava from Jang'ombe], among others.

Her Swahili songs attracted a lot of attention, and even the Sultan's wife, Sayyida Matuka, invited her to perform at the royal palace. Siti was the first artist to sing Taarab in Swahili and spread it abroad.

WOMEN'S GROUPS (1945)

In 1945, women's Taarab groups were formed, which brought exciting entertainment and attracted audiences. These groups included: Royal Air Force, Royal Navy, Bananti, Sahib el Arri and Nuru el Uyuni.

At that time, weddings were mainly entertained by women, who would sing popular songs from Arabic and Indian traditions and then insert their own lyrics. Women did not play instruments themselves; rather, men would play for them.

Women's groups had many members – sometimes even 100 in a single group. They would also support each other financially in events like weddings, funerals, or whenever problems arose.

The Establishment of Sauti ya Unguja (Voice of Unguja)

Sauti ya Unguja radio station was established in 1951 and greatly helped people to understand Arabic songs and become familiar with the music groups that were active at that time. In Mombasa, there was also Sauti ya Mvita, a radio station that played Arabic songs and Mombasa songs like "Kasha" [Chest/trunk], "Mgomba Changaraweni" [Banana Tree's small peebles], "Aziza ametoka kwangu" [Aziza has left me] etc. Mombasa was under the Sultan of Zanzibar. There were also singers performing in an Indian style like Juma Baloo, and another famous singer, Zein Al Abidin, who played the oud and was very popular.

Later, there were famous female singers like Asha Abdo Malika and Zuhura Hawa, who often used the Chakacha rhythm.

Entertainment Programs

Groups such as Nadi Ikhwan Safaa, Magoa, and artist Mr. Ali performed songs in Hindi, English, and Arabic styles like Nabole and Ghannilly.

141

Michenzani Social Club (1955)

This club was established in 1955 and quickly became popular. One of its famous artists was Bakari Abeid, who was also a renowned poet. He sang both Arabic songs and Swahili Taarab songs. His early songs had a western cha-cha rhythm, like "Njiwa peleka salamu" [Pigeon, Send my Greetings], Bakari Abeid sang many beloved love songs like "Mazoea yana tabu" [Familiarity Brings Trouble], "Kisebu sebu" [The Hustle and Bustle], "Napenda kwa ishara" [I Love Through Gestures] etc. His songs were popular because they touched people's emotions and spread throughout East Africa and the Comoros.

The music composer was Masoud Mohd Rashid, popularly known as Dr. Ayub. Another key figure was Hija Saleh, a school teacher and poet who worked alongside Masauni Yussuf. They also acted in plays used by Sauti ya Unguja and performed at venues like Rahaleo Hall.

The Origin of Culture Musical Club Zanzibar (1957)

During the political movement for independence from colonial rule in 1957, the Afro Shirazi Party (ASP), through its Youth League (ASPYL), mobilized youth to form Taarab groups and drama clubs to inspire and push for political change.

One such group was Shime Kuokoana, based in Gulioni. Its main goal was to support ASP branches by performing Taarab and using the proceeds to strengthen the party's activities. These shows were held in town and rural areas, providing both entertainment and political education.

Dramatic Society

After the 1964 Revolution, the ASPgovernment brought together all Taarab-related groups to form one entity called Dramatic Society, headquartered at Kiswandui in Wangazija's club.

After a year, it was reorganized, and a new organization called the Culture Department was created at Said Wanatepe's home (according to the book of Culture Musical Club).

Another account (by Idi A. Farhan) explains that groups were brought together under the Department of Culture and Traditions, chaired by the late Maalim Idi A. Farhan.

142

Ghazi (1960)

In the 1960s, disagreements arose within Nadi Ikhwan Safaa, leading some members to break away and form Ghazi, which became a major competitor. Ghazi's leader was Buaisha, one of the founders of nis who had studied music in Egypt. He also contributed greatly to strengthening nis.

In several competitions organized by the government, only three clubs participated: Culture Musical Club, nis, and Ghazi.

Yasu

Yasu was a youth group of ASP, prepared and trained to support the party's development. They had their own songs and allowed children to start singing.

Other Groups

Many groups emerged in Ng'ambu, gathering in the evenings to practice instruments. These included: Shime, Gulioni, Miembeni (1963, Elina), Makadara, Miti Ulaya, Kikwajuni, Mikunguni (1960), Kiembe Samaki (1960), and Kwalimsha (1963).

Later groups included: Sabri Jamil (1985), Jeshi (1986), Twinkling (1989), and Bwawani (1989).

The Independence Movement

During the fight for independence, every political party had its own artists who performed before leaders gave speeches. For example: Hizbulwatan sang songs like "Kwetu sote Mwingereza kachusha" [For All of Us, the Englishman Has Spoiled Things], "Afrika hana maisha" [Life is Hard in Africa]; Afro Shirazi Party sang songs like "Shime Shime" [Let's Get Moving!].

Taarab Groups after the Revolution

After the Revolution, there were major changes in Taarab groups and radio broadcasts. The radio changed from Sauti ya Unguja to Sauti ya Tanzania Zanzibar. Love songs were banned, and only songs praising the government and promoting patriotism were allowed.

This led many people to stop listening to Radio Zanzibar and turn to mainland Tanzania stations for news and announcements.

All Taarab groups were gathered under the Afro Shirazi Party. For example: NIS became Malindi ASP; Ghazi became Muembe

143

Tanga ASP. Other groups were named after their neighborhoods, like Mikunguni ASP etc.

All were united under one umbrella group for the arts, chaired by Maalim Iddi Abdalla Farhan. A national group was formed, bringing together top artists from various groups. Likewise, Tanzania formed its own national group, including Alwatan, Egyptian, etc.

Arabic rhythms like Wahed Unus Sharha2 were abandoned in favor of local rhythms like Tutulanga, Unyago, Rumba, Samba etc.

Later, clubs were allowed to use their original names again, like Nadi Ikhwan Safaa, but the name Ghazi was no longer used – they continued as Muembe Tanga.

Culture Musical Club

This group was formed in 1985 when all groups were consolidated under ASP. Culture Musical Club has traveled to many countries, educates, and supports many artists.

Ilyas Twinkling Stars

This group was founded in 1989 and was famous for its musical style and talented musicians. They were invited to perform in countries like France, Japan, and Italy. It was founded by Professor Mohammed Ilyas.

Kithara

This is a group that travels widely, led by Rajab Suleiman, an expert in playing the qanun.

Tausi

This was the first all-women Taarab group where the artists played their own instruments. This female orchestra was formed in 2009. They performed in events organized by the African Union, Egypt, Beirut, Mayotte, and various un events in Zanzibar and mainland Tanzania.

Bi Kidude

144 Tausi Women's Taarab Orchestra also featured guest star Bi Kidude the undisputed queen of Taarab and Unyago music and also a protégé of Siti binti Saad – the mother of Taarab. Bi Kidude was born in the village of Mfagimaringo in colonial Zanzibar.

Bi Kidude's exact date of birth is unknown; much of her life story is uncorroborated, giving her an almost mythical status. In her 90s and still the island's leading exponent of the ancient dance rituals, her many talents were acknowledged by Zanzibar International Film Festival at the second Festival of the Dhow countries in 1999.

In 2005 Bi Kidude received the lifetime achievement Womex Award for her outstanding contribution to music and culture in Zanzibar.

Uwaridi Female Band

A group that plays both music and drums, including Taarab. It was formed by female students who met at the DCMA music school.

Rahatul Zaman

This group strives to promote and preserve traditional Taarab, although it mainly performs songs from various groups.

Tabasam

Founded by Mohammed Othman, who also runs a music school at Ngome Kongwe for teaching traditional Taarab to new learners.

G Cleff

G Cleff is a Taarab group founded by Issa Matona, from Zanzibar. The group was formed to develop and modernize Taarab music while preserving its Zanzibari roots. Known for its unique style combining traditional and modern instruments, G Cleff also involves youth in Taarab music. Through this group, Matona has shown great creativity and contributed to Taarab's evolution and the preservation of Zanzibar's musical heritage.

Taarab Album Records

The record production of The Music of Zanzibar series marks a significant chapter in the preservation and global recognition of Zanzibar's rich musical heritage. The project, first initiated by Ben Mandelson in 1987, began when he approached Mariam Hamdani with the idea of compiling and recording the diverse sounds of Zanzibar. Mariam

145

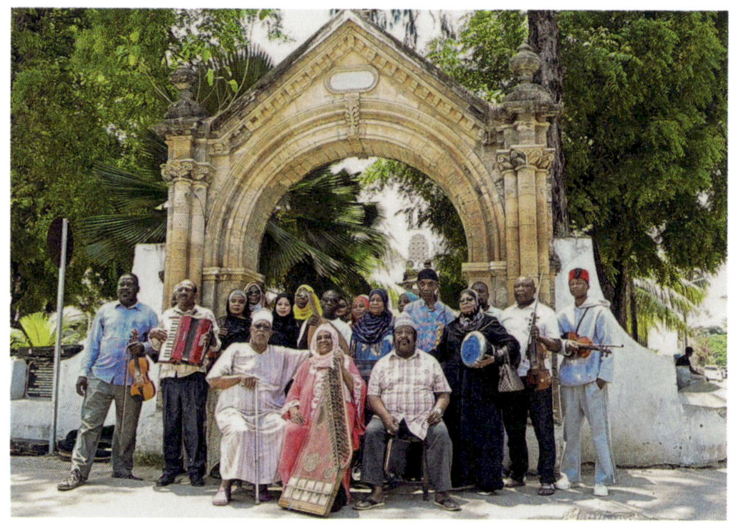

© Sauti Za Busara, 2025.

played a crucial role in coordinating the project, bringing together musicians from various backgrounds. The first album featured the talents of Seif Salim Saleh and Abdullah Mussa Ahmed, highlighting their mastery in traditional Taarab music. The second album showcased the iconic Ikhwan Safaa Musical Club, one of the oldest and most respected Taarab groups in Zanzibar. The third album, released later, was particularly special as it brought together musicians from different groups – a rare collaboration that captured the collective spirit of Zanzibari music. It was in this album that Bi Kidude, already a respected local figure, began to gain wider recognition for her powerful voice and charismatic presence. The fourth and final album in the series featured the celebrated Culture Musical Club, further cementing the legacy of The Music of Zanzibar project as an essential documentation of the island's musical tradition.

Zanzibar Traditional Taarab Association (Taarab Heritage Ensemble)

This is an association that brings together eight traditional Taarab groups, both large and small. These include: Nadi Ikhwan Safaa (NIS), Culture Musical Club; Tausi; Uwaridi; Tabasam; Kithara; Nyota za Meremeta; and G Cleff.

The Contribution Of Busara, Ziff, and Emerson Foundation

These organizations have been very instrumental in promoting and strengthening Taarab music both locally and internationally.

Through festivals such as Zanzibar International Film Festival and Sauti za Busara, traditional Taarab groups have had excellent opportunities to showcase their talent. Some groups have even been lucky enough to receive invitations to perform abroad after being seen at these festivals.

Apart from performing, these festivals also offer artists the chance to meet, network, and exchange ideas with artists from other groups.

DCMA, Mohamed Othman Music School, Culture Musical Club, Malindi, and Tausi

All these institutions help in teaching, nurturing, and developing many students and artists in the country, playing a key role in preserving traditional Taarab music.

BASFFU (Council for National Arts, Film, and Culture)

This is a council established to oversee all matters related to culture in Zanzibar.

COSOZA (Copyright Society of Zanzibar)

This is an organization established by the government to help protect the rights of artists and their creative works.

Application for the Inscription of Traditional Taarab in Unesco's World Heritage List

The Zanzibar Traditional Taarab Association has submitted a request to the Honorable Minister responsible for Culture, seeking for traditional Taarab to be inscribed in UNESCO's World Heritage List.

1   Narrated and written by Shaibu Abeid Barajab – Archival Documents.
2   Literally "One/Two/Expansion," the expression may refer to a ternary rhythmic pattern or a call-and-response framework used in Taarab or Arabic-influenced music.

Invocations:

Territory, Intimacy, and the Intangible

Conversation with
Bonaventure Soh Bejeng Ndikung

Thiago de Paula Souza: Let's go back to the basics. Now that we're working together in a different context and framework – and the *Invocations* have been reimagined, and twisted, I'd like you to reflect and try to imagine when the idea, the notion of "invocation" first came to you. I'd like to return to day one. Did the first ones emerge during your time at SAVVY? When and how did it first take shape in your mind?

Bonaventure Soh Bejeng Ndikung: To trully go back, we'd need to return about fifteen years, to the early days of SAVVY, which began in 2009. We had just started organizing exhibitions, but it quickly became clear that exhibitions alone weren't enough. We felt the need to activate discourse in other ways. The idea of the *Invocations* emerged from this: as a form of public programming, as a way of gathering around certain ideas and calling something forth – invoking something. It wasn't just that we felt a conference or symposium, where people come and present talks, was insufficient. We wanted to create a space where ideas could be called upon – those present in the space, and those absent; spirits and presences that are there, and others that are beyond. The intention has always been to activate what lies beyond the visible – working simultaneously with the visible and the invisible.[1] To me, the *Invocation* is really about rethinking how we write history – pushing beyond the limits of traditional historiography. If conventional history is written by excavating archives that are visible and tangible, how can we engage with archives that are not?

Take, for instance, our work in Zanzibar with Taarab. Of course, we can reference the songs composed in 1958, 1963, and so on, but what we're really dealing with is everything that surrounds them – the affective, the ephemeral, the intangible. That's what the *Invocation* allows us to access.

TdPS: Since you mentioned Taarab and Zanzibar, let me pick up on that thread. When you first began conceptualizing the *Invocations*, was sound/the sonic already an important element?

BSBN: The sonic has always been essential to every *Invocation* I've done. For me, sonic space is one of the richest archival spaces. When I speak of rethinking historiography, I mean also rethinking the politics of reference, of source-making. Music becomes a critical source – a space where knowledge is held, where stories can be told from different vantage points. Music is a bridge between this world and what lies beyond. If we want to connect with that which is not tangible or visible, not recorded in conventional forms, then we need the sonic. The sonic invokes and

149

evokes things we cannot see but can feel. Poetry, the sonic, and the body – performativity. As Esiaba Irobi said, the body is a site of discourse. These three – poetry, sound, and the body – are the main vessels of *Invocation*. Then come the lectures, the keynote talks. But equally essential are the performances, the singing, the poetry, the improvisation, which plays a central role.

> **TdPS:** Improvisation is also one of the main topics of our conversation in Zanzibar. But before going to improvisation, I wonder if we could focus a little bit more on your first encounter with that land. We have always been careful in how to establish a proximity with a territory, and not being flying saucers… During the past months we've been discussing ways of creating intimacy with the places we are travelling to.

BSBN: So for each of the sites where we went to, it was very important that we work with people from there, people on the ground, people that are connected to these spaces. I like the idea of intimacy, it's actually the politics of intimacy. Actually a major issue with many events organized in different contexts – you end up landing there like a kind of UFO, completely disconnected from the context. That's something we've always tried to avoid. One way we've addressed this – going back to my collaborations with SAVVY, for example – has been by working closely with people on the ground, those who truly understand the local context. It reminds me of how Patrick Chamoiseau talks about Édouard Glissant writing from and about the Caribbean islands: rooted in place, shaped by lived experience. He says when the Europeans came, they built roads, they built these big structures, you know, which were very predictable, which were roads leading to the sea, you know, railways leading to the sea to tap resources from the inland and bring them directly there. But Chamboiseau says something very interesting, he says, but before the Europeans came and even when the Europeans came and were there, and even when they left, there was something that he calls *traces*. So the people from the land, the indigenous had all these roads that were there, that were not visible to the eyes of the colonizers. So when you talk about intimacy, that's what is evoked in me. How do we find those *traces*? To be able to find those *traces*, we need to work with people that come from those communities, that understand the space, that recognize these traces and can walk these paths, right?

So with each *Invocation*, we're trying not to walk the main roads. So when Conceição Evaristo still says "not all travelers walk roads," what paths do these travelers take? Roads are the colonial structures or the patriarchal structures or the structures that are imposed upon us, the violent structures that we see in the world. Traces are the other spaces that the travelers take.

TdPS: But traces can disappear.

BSBN: And that is very interesting, which is also fine. But we must engage in two things. We must engage in the finding of the traces that are there and that have disappeared. And we must engage in the creation of new traces.

TdPS: But then this also demands some sort of, I'm repeating myself, but it demands some sort of intimacy. Because that's the only way to find a trace.

BSBN: Yes. So intimacy comes with knowledge about space and time and engaging with a certain poetics. Conceição Evaristo says "there are submerged worlds that only the silence of poetry penetrates"… To me, that's how we get into those traces. To me, that is what intimacy means. The silence of poetry. When you get to that space, then you can find your way into those traces. You can find your way into those submerged worlds. But to do that, you have to invoke something. It is not done by cognition alone. You don't get to those spaces by only the knowledge you learned in universities. No. You need a certain form of affect and affection to be able to get into those spaces. That's why I'm interested in exhibition making. Because it's a space of affect. It's a space of deep understanding. It's embodied cognition. Your whole body thinks with you to be able to find those traces.

To answer concretely, if you take the case of Zanzibar, the only way we could do it really was to work with Ben, who comes from the inner country, but he lives in Dar es Salaam and he knows Zanzibar very well. To work with people like Khamis and all the other people at the Dao Country Music Academy (DCM), and so on.[2] These are people who live and work in Stone Town, who think with and through the sonic landscape of the place – not only as an epistemological space, but also as a historiographic one. It's a space of heritage. They understand that the stones hold the memory of the place, just as much as the sounds do. And the only way to create real intimacy with that context was to be able to lean on those stones – both literally and metaphorically – and to lean into, or even embody, the music that resonates from them.

 TdPS: You first visited Tanzania through Dar es Salaam. Can we revisit that moment – what was happening during your time there? After that visit, did you already have a sense that an *Invocation* might one day take place in that context?

BSBN: It was a very particular and powerful moment. We chose to go to Dar es Salaam because, in the late 1960s and early 1970s, Walter Rodney was teaching at the University of Dar es Salaam. Around that same period, *Cheche*, a significant leftist magazine, was founded there by a group of scholars engaged in liberation movements. We were working on a project centered around Walter Rodney's *How Europe Underdeveloped Africa* – a fundamental book.[3] We were there to commemorate the 50th anniversary of its publication, reflecting on the concepts of development and underdevelopment, and more importantly, on how to imagine and exist in a post-underdevelopment era. We were asking: how can we move beyond the binary classification of the world into "developed" and "underdeveloped"?

It was a remarkable historical moment, and so the SAVVY team,[4] along with Frank Herman Ekra and several invited guests from around the world, came together in that context to honor and reflect on these legacies. From Pakistan, Germany, Cameroon, and Colombia – we all came together in Dar es Salaam to carry out this work. While there, we collaborated closely with Ben and Jesse Gerard Mpango, who lead the Ajabu Ajabu,[5] the institution that hosted us.

They research through film and bring filmic work to the people.. We could do it at the university, but we wanted to do it with them. Because to us, again, going back to the politics of intimacy, their institution works this way. They would go out to the street, hang bed sheets and project a film on it. And people would come and watch. And there's going to be a discussion afterward. So we wanted to work like that.

> **TdPS:** Often people are just more attached to the visual, but films are also sonic vessels of knowledge. But what about the decision to go to Zanzibar?

BSBN: Precisely. So that was my entry into Dar es Salaam. And it was fantastic because we got to know so many people. I remember doing an interview with a guy called John Kitime, who's a music specialist from Tanzania. And we're talking about the different music genres. And he told me, to understand Taraab, you have to go to Zanzibar. I was asking him all these questions. He said, you have to go there. So to me, it was just in my mind. Then, of course, I forgot about it. And then during the preparations for Bienal de Sao Paulo, when we were trying to decide where the *Invocations* could happen it felt to me we had to go to Zanzibar.

Thinking of the connection to water and to connection to the sonic and the question of conjugating humanity within different spaces.

> **TdPS:** Let's talk more about our partners there. Of course, we already mentioned Ben, but I would like us to talk more about the school, DCMA, and the Young Stars. Shall we maybe talk more about the encounter with them? Their performances, your impression of the young musicians.
>
> And that's just like a way for us to talk about Taraab in a certain sense. Because what was suspicious at first and for me was also the most exciting thing is that I didn't encounter a dead tradition or culture. I didn't encounter something that belonged to the past that was only fascinating to outsiders. I could see something very alive and reinventing itself. Maybe we can use Taraab now as a metaphor to think about encounters between the contemporary and the tradition.

BSBN: So it wasn't my first time working with the DCMA. I don't know if you know that. So I've worked with them a few years ago. And when Natasha Ginwala and I did this exhibition called *Indigo Waves and Other Stories*,[6] we invited them to be part of the exhibition we did in Berlin.

We commissioned, I think, a one hour composition from the students and faculty of the DCMA. You know, because we're thinking about what is called the Indian Ocean, what we call the Swahili Sea. You know, as a space of convergence of cultures. So the idea of this project, *Indigo Waves and Other Stories*, was really to shift the attention from the Atlantic and to think of the relation between the African continent and the Gulf and the Indian subcontinent.

> **TdPS:** It's a different perspective for us to encounter the African continent. That's when we're talking from, let's say, Brazil.

BSBN: Exactly. So what we know is the Black Atlantic; as you know, US-American universities have pumped in a lot of money. So this is talked about, the African diaspora on this side of the world is very well known, very well discussed, very well studied. We're interested in that relationship, which during the Unesco gathering, in 1974,[7] about the Indian Ocean, it was called the oldest continent in human history. You know, because you could step on a dhow or some other boat and the winds will carry you from East Africa to India and all the way around. The technologies of people moving from East Africa to India and back for thousands and thousands of years.

153

TdPS: And it's like such a powerful and beautiful image. Because it's also something when I saw those boats – of course, they're different now. But still, I was thinking, how brave one needs to be.

BSBN: But they had incredible technologies. The boats were very simple, but very sophisticated. The sails and so on, the incredible technologies. Now, the DCMA does something very interesting and very unique. They're doing a different form of mapping. They're not mapping based on land.

You say, okay, we are from East Africa, so we accept East Africans. Or we are from the Sahel, so we accept people from the Sahel. No, they say the countries that are related to the Dhow. It's a different way of mapping. So countries that use this boat. You go to the Gulf, people use this kind of boat. You go to East Africa, people use this boat. When you go to the Indian subcontinent, people use this boat. And so based on this form of mapping, they created an academy.

TdPS: And that's, I mean, when you say it's an alternative way of mapping or another way of mapping, what excites me is that it forces us to relate, to create different relations between countries. Relations that are not based on their, I don't know, colonial resources.

BSBN: Yes, you know, exactly. That's what they do. Which I find fascinating. So it's a form of relationality. So they've put that together. So now, one thing, one of the ways in which these countries manifest their relation is through music. Because, and the music is Taraab. Because in Taraab you find cultures from the Indian subcontinent, from East Africa, from the Gulf, and so on and so forth. They all come together there. And it's fascinating. So they use that, they founded this school as a possibility of preserving this music, this heritage, this intangible but very important heritage. And that's how I got to know Halda, Khamis, and so on and so forth, you know, through this composition.

TdPS: And how can we work also in such a changing landscape. Not only the natural landscape is changing, but also the massive presence of all the tourists.

BSBN: Yes, that is true. But at the same time, it is still there. You and I went to that forest. I've never been to a forest with corals. Never. So it is true that it's changing. And you have all these stories.

TdPS: That's true.

BSBN: At the same time, there is a fast time of all these stories coming and passing and leaving. And there's a slow time of the corals being there for millions of years. So that forest was once upon a time the bottom of the sea. So you have the corals in your face. Those same corals were used, coral stones were used to build the Stone Town. So you have it in your face. So that to me is the slow time. Right? So everything is going fast, but it's still there.

And that's one thing I very much liked about being there, experiencing the fast pace of things, but being grounded by the slowness of it. You see people just sitting there, you know, doing what you call in the Caribbean, sliming. Just being. Slow time. The tourists are running up and down, but these guys are slow. And there's power in that. There's beauty in it. Just like the stones.

> **TdPS:** I guess what also stayed with me, like encountering those corals, like seeing those rocks on the ground, was that even if one is not open to that, you encounter something beyond human. Yes. You're forced to encounter something beyond human history.

BSBN: Yes, yes, yes.

> **TdPS:** Or something that is really, we can say, as you mentioned, like slow time, or a notion like the relationality that happens beyond human communities.

BSBN: But that is why we do *Invocations*, you know, we do *Invocations* because we want to be portals through which those things that happen beyond human communities can flow through us. So, the *Invocation* is a possibility of making yourself receptive to the voice of the stone, to the stories that the stones, the corals can tell.

> **TdPS:** And the corals in a certain sense, they also become the traces that you mentioned before. Or you need someone to help you learn about them.

BSBN: Precisely. Because they are there, but one might not see them at first. You need to have someone teach you about them. So they're there, they're present, the stones are speaking, but you must be, you must have the sensibility of listening to them to be able to hear them. You must be receptive to it, to be able to hear them.

And that is why we chose the idea of improvisation there, because improvisation is the possibility of opening up oneself and allowing for a vocabulary that is not processed by cognition to flow through you. So it's not just the head that is speaking, but the whole body, the spine, and so forth. So to be able to be the vessel through which the sound of the stones, these coral stones can express themselves, you have to open up that space of improvisation.

So that's why we chose the Mawali and the Taqsim as possibilities for thinking about Taraab. So the instrumental improvisation and the voice improvisation. So really, when you just start singing, you allow for all…

So there's a moment in the 36th Bienal curatorial statement where we cite Leo Asemota when he asks: when you look at the mirror, who do you see? And he answers himself: you see all the people that came before you and the people that accompany you. So improvisation does something similar. So when you set yourself into that space, you see that all the voices that came before you, the human beings and the non-human beings can flow through you. So that becomes possible through improvisation in Taraab.

> **TdPS:** Something that is important to the core of the *Invocations* is the notion of no nation-states. Even if we're looking to those territories, to those cities, to those villages, to those locations we tried to expand the conversation from the limits of the nation-states.
>
> This is the reason why it's so important to map relations between regions that go beyond the historically established or the most conventional ones. The example
>
> Something that was interesting to hear, in fact to listen to, was when you mentioned Farrokhzad's poem, "Only Voices Remain."[8] And you read it and I wanted to hear you saying more again about what remains after one *Invocation* is finished. I'll go back to the beginning of our conversation, beyond what is tangible, what remains?

BSBN: Oh, that's a beautiful question. And I'm very happy you mentioned Forugh Farrokhzad. You know, somewhere in the poem she says something, a sentence which I'm using as the title of my next book. Somewhere she says something about seeping. I found it extremely beautiful. Voice seeping into time. That's the title of my next book. I thought it was so beautiful. So the question of what remains can only be answered by this. The voices, the music seeping into time, seeping into the slow time of the stone, of the growth of the stone, a very slow time. You know, the voice seeping into the slow time of the people hanging out there in the dhows, you know, just chilling, the kids dancing and doing gymnastics all day long across the seaside.

It's also about the fact that not only the kids, but the older people like Professor Mohamed Ilyas, you know, that normally do not meet these kids, or Mama Mariam Hamdani, that normally do, that these people could come together and could think together, they could sing. You could, you know, there was so much, you know, you remember when he started crying there, there was so much emotion.

So what remains is the affection created through music and through the knowledge and the history shared in that space. To me, that intangible memory created, first of all, the intangible memory evoked, invoked, and the intangible memory that stays there is something that remains. The fact that, you know, these people are now working on ways of doing new albums, collaborations. Without this conference, without this *Invocation*, maybe they wouldn't have done that, you know. So this kind of intergenerational encounters.

1   The concept of the *Invocation* has also happened in other contexts such as *Sonsbeek, Bamako Encounters,* or the *Finland Pavilion* in 2019.
2   Bernard Ntahondi and Khamis Muhamed Juma were co-conveners of *Invocation* #3.
3   Walter Rodney, *How Europe Underdeveloped Africa* (1972). London and New York: Verso, 2018.
4   More info about the project at https://savvy-contemporary.com/en/projects/2024/unraveling-the-under-development-complex/. Accessed in Apr. 2025.
5   See more at https://ajabuajabu.com/Audio-Visual-House. Accessed in Apr. 2025.
6   *Indigo Waves and Other Stories: Re-Navigating the Afrasian Sea and Notions of Diaspora*. Gropius Bau, Berlin, from Apr. 6th to Aug. 13th, 2023. More at https://www.berlinerfestspiele.de/en/gropius-bau/programm/2023/ausstellungen/indigo-waves. Accessed in Apr. 2025.
7   See: "Historical Relations Across the Indian Ocean". *The General Histories of Africa: Studies and Documents*, v. 3, no. 14, 1980. Available at https://unesdoc.unesco.org/ark:/48223/pf0000042152. Accessed in May, 2025.
8   See pp. 28-29 of this book.

Mawali–Taqsim: Improvisation as a Space and Technology of Humanity

Bernard Ntahondi

It is an immense honor to be part of this moment, to stand among visionaries, creators, and thinkers gathered under the conceptual brilliance of Bonaventure Soh Bejeng Ndikung and the team behind the 36th Bienal de São Paulo. This Bienal, a space of convergence, pushes beyond the traditional boundaries of art and scholarship, urging us to interrogate, reimagine, and embody humanity as a living, evolving practice.

This edition of the Bienal, through its *Invocations*, shifts our understanding of humanity from a noun to a verb, an active process, an engagement, an improvisation. In Zanzibar, where we gathered, this perspective found profound resonance. This is a place where cultures have intersected for centuries, where languages blend, where melodies from distant shores fuse into something singular yet plural. It is here that we confront the layered histories of migration, trade, colonialism, and resistance, and it is here that we listen, through music, to the rhythms of survival, adaptation, and improvisation.

Dunia Rangi Mbili:
The Dualities of Existence

Haji Gora Haji and Khamis Abeid's song "Dunia Rangi Mbili" [The World Has Two Colors] reminds us that the world is never singular. It is, by its nature, layered, contradictory, and in constant flux. This "two-faced world" speaks to the perpetual dance between joy and sorrow, harmony and discord, freedom and constraint. But the wisdom embedded in this phrase does not urge us to accept duality as a simple binary. Rather, it compels us to go further, to embrace complexity, to see beyond rigid divisions, and to recognize the richness that emerges when multiple perspectives, histories, and traditions coexist.

This multiplicity is nowhere more evident than in the tradition of Taarab, a music form that defies categorization, a sonic archive of movement and exchange. Taarab carries within it the echoes of Africa, the Middle East, South Asia, and Europe. It is a reminder that culture is not static, that identity is not singular, and that humanity itself is an improvisational act, one that is continually reconfigured, reimagined, and reborn.

Improvisation as a Technology of Humanity

Improvisation is often understood as spontaneity, a deviation from the script. But in the context of Taarab, and indeed in the broader context of human existence, improvisation is much more than that. It is a form of knowledge, a mode of survival, a technology of adaptation. It is how stories are told, how traditions evolve, how resilience is practiced.

In Taarab, improvisation occurs in multiple forms. It is present in the way musicians respond to one another, in the way singers reshape lyrics to reflect the moment, in the way audiences interact with performances. It is a living, breathing process, an art form that refuses to be confined.

This extends beyond music. Improvisation is deeply embedded in the social and political realities of Zanzibar and the broader Swahili Coast. It is seen in the way communities navigate shifting political landscapes, in the ways language adapts and absorbs, in the ways history is remembered and retold. Improvisation is not simply about creating something new; it is about making space for fluidity, for movement, for reconfiguration.

To improvise is to recognize the unpredictability of life and to respond with creativity and agency. It is an act of defiance against rigidity and an assertion of possibility. In the Swahili world, where histories of colonialism and resistance intersect, improvisation has been and continues to be a vital force.

Zanzibar as a Model of Multiplicity

Zanzibar's history is one of encounters. It has been a place of trade and conquest, of migration and settlement, of struggle and resilience. Its very essence is shaped by its openness to the world, by its ability to absorb and transform. This multiplicity is reflected in its architecture, its language, its cuisine, and, most vividly, in its music.

Taarab embodies this openness. It is neither wholly African, nor Arab, nor Indian, nor European. It is all of these and more. It carries the histories of those who have passed through Zanzibar's shores, the joys and sorrows of those who have called this place home. It is, in many ways, an auditory archive of a multi-faced humanity.

In a world that often seeks to impose rigid boundaries between nations, cultures and identities, Zanzibar offers a different model. It demonstrates that coexistence does not require homogeneity, that difference need not lead to division. It reminds us that humanity thrives not in isolation, but in connection, in exchange, in improvisation.

Art as Liberation: The Role of Music and Improvisation

Music, and indeed all art, has long been a site of liberation. It is through music that silences are broken, that histories are reclaimed, that futures are imagined. Taarab, with its layered meanings and fluid structures, is particularly powerful in this regard. It gives voice to personal and collective experiences, it creates space for critique, and it offers a form of resistance against imposed narratives.

Improvisation, as seen in Taarab, teaches us that freedom is not found in fixed forms but in the ability to adapt, to shift, to respond. It is a practice of agency, of claiming space in a world that often seeks to dictate and control. It is an act of self-determination.

161

As we reflect on this, we must also consider our own roles. How do we, as artists, curators, and thinkers, engage with improvisation? How do we embrace the unscripted in our own work? How do we create spaces where multiplicity is not just acknowledged but celebrated?

A Call to Conjugate Humanity

On this journey of *Invocation* #3, let us take inspiration from Taarab and from the traditions of improvisation that define Zanzibar. Let us see improvisation not merely as a technique but as a way of being in the world, an approach that values openness, fluidity, and possibility.

Let us conjugate humanity not as a fixed state but as an ongoing process. Let us move beyond rigid definitions and instead embrace the richness of multiplicity. Let us recognize that to be human is not a static condition but an active, evolving practice one that requires listening, adapting, and creating.

And as we gather here, in celebration of this art form, let us leave not only inspired but also committed to carrying forward its message of unity, creativity, and hope. Let us allow the music to guide us, the words to inspire us, and the spirit of Zanzibar to remind us that humanity, at its best, is an improvisational act.

Asanteni sana. Asalam aleykum.

Territory of Improvisation among Tides, Memories and Encounters

Keyna Eleison

Africasiamerica

No setor tropical do mundo
As belezas se derramam
As belezas se derramam
Sob o sol quente, sangue quente
Está a mostra em cada
esquina mas tudo é tão bonito,
Mas tudo é tão bonito
Africasiamerica tranquila
Africasiamerica tranquila
Negro, branco amarelo meu céu
O som da tua festa me alucina
Eis o meu abraço sem fel
Mire irmão, estamos com você
Sem cansar, sem cansar amor
Mire irmão, lutamos por você
Sem parar, sem parar amor
Love for all
Love for all
[In the tropical sector
of the world
The beauties spill out
The beauties spill out
Under the hot sun, hot blood
It's on display around every
corner but everything is so beautiful,
But everything is so beautiful
tranquil Africasiamerica
tranquil Africasiamerica
Black, white yellow my sky
The sound of your party makes me hallucinate
Here's my embrace without gall
Look brother, we're with you
Without tiring, without tiring love
 Look brother, we're fighting for you
Without stopping, without stopping love
Love for all
Love for all]

165 **Gonzaguinha**, 1968

Improvisation, as a technology of humanity, pulsates from within, it reveals a vital space of profound and historical encounters, where interaction, listening, and exchange become tools for collective construction, a gesture that transcends time and geography, weaving together affect, knowledge, and memory. It emerges as an instinctive response, a whisper that bows to the present and reinvents the instant.

There is a possibility of a territory of improvisation – a real island shaped by metaphor, where traveled feet, calloused hands, and experienced bodies meet and create. It is no idyllic paradise in practice, but a space surrounded by water on all sides, enveloped by force on all sides. There, improvisation is built on the tension between resistance and renewal; it is stone and wind, rock and foam. Each sound generated in this insular territory bears the marks of the bodies that go through the experience and imprint their pain, their power, and their memories upon it. Improvisation is formed as a technique of encounter, where the gesture of the other becomes an invitation and error is transformed into creation.

This island, which vibrates like a collective body, is Zanzibar – this ancient stage for encounters and interchanges. There, the land always seems to be by the sea, and the air carries the voices of travelers, merchants, pilgrims, and outcasts. In Zanzibar, this gesture manifests itself in the sonorous skin of the Taarab, a music that is also narrative, prayer, and rebellion. The Taarab is more than a melody; it is a form of invocation, an expanded listening that becomes a collective body.

Taarab is born from this intersection – a web of sound where Arab, African, Indian, and Western influences intertwine. It spreads out like a carpet woven from the threads of collective memories, where each note carries the weight and lightness of the encounters that generated it.

Improvising in the world of Taarab is a practice of intense listening. The musicians move like acrobats, attentive to each other's gestures, playing between the predictable and the unexpected. The instruments: the *kanun* (sitar), the *oud* (lute) and the violin converse as if speaking a secret language, translating silences and pauses. The intense, wailing voices weave together words that can be prayers or provocations, truths or riddles. The improvised lyrics are often released as arrows – sharp, comic or devastating – reverberating in a code that only the immediate audience can decipher.

Improvising in the Taarab is also a way of conjuring up absences, of making present what has disappeared. The voices that rise up echo the silences of the lives erased by the trafficking of enslaved people, by colonial violence, by the stories that remained on the margins. Improvisation is a technology that tears time apart. Time finds in improvisation a form of restitution, an echo of justice.

On stage or in the streets, time dilates during a Taarab performance. The notes seem to lengthen, as if they wanted to merge with the salty breeze that invades Zanzibar. Sometimes the musician falls silent and the audience calls him back, offering their voices as a conduit for him to return to the song. At other times, it's the singer who pauses and, in the empty space, we only hear the murmurs of the sea. This vacuum is also part of the improvisation – a suspension that invites full presence.

Improvising is an art of survival, a strategy of resistance and invention. Zanzibar, with its winding streets and shade-covered courtyards, carries the memory of this gesture. Each beat of the drum, each vibration of the string, each inflection of the voice retraces the path of peoples who crossed oceans, who resisted erasure through sound and song. Improvising is weaving the present with the threads of past lives. Improvisation in Taarab is not just an aesthetic resource, but a field of political and affective negotiation. The intensity of the gaze, the unexpected pause or the vocal inflection reveal a subterranean communication, where pacts and silent understandings are built.

This process connects to a broader tradition of improvisation as a fundamental practice of humanity. In times of crisis, displacement, or invisibility, the ability to create from the present – to transform a gesture, a word, or a sound into a new proposition – emerges as a powerful technique for survival and reinvention. Zanzibar, whose history has been marked by the trafficking of enslaved people, commercial influences, and migratory flows, offers a territoriality where this technology is deeply embedded. The Taarab, in its improvised brilliance, reminds us that humanity has always found a place of power in the unpredictable. In Zanzibar, this practice rises up as a poetics of the instant, where sound and silence mingle, and where the encounter is transformed into living history. There, improvisation is a formula for permanence, a secret that reveals that humanity, when it listens and takes risks, always finds a new way of reinventing itself. With its sinuous melodies and verses that meander between love, politics, and everyday life, it is the result of a vast tangle of cultural influences. In Zanzibar, an island that stands as a meeting point between Africa, Asia, and the Middle East, Taarab manifests itself as a sound cartography of historical crossings. It incorporates Arabic scales, African rhythms, Indian harmonies, and Western elements, creating a soundscape that is not fixed, but expands in improvised flows.

At the intersection where oceans meet, the Taarab remains a reflection of this web of encounters. It states that improvising is also digging into one's own history, absorbing influences and returning them in the form of sound, gesture, or words.

167

Improvisation, as a technology of humanity, allows the past to resonate in the present and the now to project itself into the future, forever porous to the presences that cross its paths.

> *Admiro os cantos que são curvas*
> *Observo Aprendo*
> *Vejo quem me vê Danço e aprendo*
> *Percorrer é viver todo dia...*
> *E assim, cada parar é uma construção de ritmo.*

> *[I admire the corners that are curves*
> *I watch*
> *I learn*
> *I see who sees me*
> *I dance and learn*
> *To travel is to live every day...*
> *And so each halt is a construction of rhythm.]*

About the
authors

Aisha Bakary (Hijab DJ) is a trail-blazing music producer and DJ celebrated as the first female DJ from Zanzibar. Born in 1995 on Pemba Island, she grew up in Unguja, where her passion for music was ignited at an early age. Deeply inspired by the rhythms of Taraab music she loved as a child, her journey into the music world would later make her a pioneer in the industry.

Ajíṭẹnà Marco Scarassatti is an ọmọ awo Ifá, educator, and artist of listening, working as a composer, sound artist, and improviser. He is a professor of musical composition at UFMG and the author of the book *Walter Smetak, o alquimista dos sons.* He coordinated the course Formação Intercultural para Educadores Indígenas (FIEI FaE UFMG) and has developed the artistic research projects *Orixás Sonoros e Escutas do fim do mundo: Música e Arte Sonora no Antropoceno.*

Allan da Rosa is a writer of fiction, theater, theory, and essays. An *Angoleiro* dancer, historian, and art educator, he also holds a master's and doctorate in Imagination, Culture, and Education from the University of São Paulo (USP). He completed his post-doctoral studies in aesthetics at the University of Cologne, Germany. Among other books, he is the author of *Balanço afiado – Estética e política em Jorge Ben* (2023, co-authored with Deivison Faustino), *Ninhos e revides – Estéticas e fundamentos, lábias e jogo de corpo* (2022), *Águas de homens pretos – Imaginário, cisma e cotidiano ancestral em São Paulo* (2021), and *Pedagoginga, autonomia e mocambagem* (2018).

Alya Sebti is a contemporary art curator and director of the ifa-Galerie (Institut für Auslandsbeziehungen) in Berlin, where she initiated the research and exhibition platform *Untie to Tie – On Colonial Legacies in Contemporary Societies*. She was co-curator of the European biennial Manifesta in Marseille (2020), guest curator of the Dakar Biennale (2018), and artistic director of the Marrakech Biennale (2014). She has led curatorial research through mentorship programs at the ZK/U artist residency (Berlin) and at MACAAL (Marrakech).

Anna Roberta Goetz is a curator and writer. She has worked at the Marta Herford Museum and the MMK Museum für Moderne Kunst Frankfurt. She was assistant curator and project manager of the German Pavilion at the 55th Venice Biennale (2013). She has organized major solo and group exhibitions in various countries and has taught at several international art academies, including the Zurich University of the Arts and the Städelschule in Frankfurt. Her publications include *Rodney McMillian: The Land: Not Without a Politic*, co-edited with Kathleen Rahn (2024), and *Cinthia Marcelle – By Means of Doubt*, co-edited with Isabella Rjeille (2023).

Bernard Ntahondi is a professional specialized in film curation and heritage management. He is currently a curator at the Dar es Salaam Center for Architectural Heritage, where he integrates his knowledge of architecture and history into his film-related endeavors.

Bi Mariam Hamdani is an accomplished journalist, musician, and cultural advocate. After retiring, Mariam used her pension to purchase musical instruments, often second-hand, and became the first woman in Zanzibar to play the qanun instrument publicly. In 2009, she founded Tausi Women's Taarab (meaning "Peacock"), Zanzibar's first all-woman Taarab orchestra. This group delivers performances of Swahili Taarab music, revolutionizing a traditionally male-dominated art form. Mariam also serves as the Chairperson of the Taarab Association, which includes seven Taarab groups in Zanzibar.

Bonaventure Soh Bejeng Ndikung is a curator, author, and biotechnologist, currently serving as the director and chief curator of the Haus der Kulturen der Welt (HKW) in Berlin. He is the founder and former artistic director of SAVVY Contemporary in Berlin, as well as the artistic director of sonsbeek (Arnhem). He is a professor and head of faculty in the Master's program in Spatial Strategies at the weißensee academy of art berlin. His published works include, among others, *The Delusions of Care* (2021), *An Ongoing-Offcoming Tale: Ruminations on Art, Culture, Politics and Us/Others* (2022), and Pidginization as Curatorial Method (2023).

DCMA Young Stars
See pp. 68-69.

Halda Mohamed Alkanaan is the Managing Director of the Dhow Countries Music Academy (DCMA). She completed various courses at the diploma level in administration management, entrepreneurship, accountancy, and arts management. Before discovering her passion for art management and joining the DCMA in 2004, as Administrator/Accountant, she worked as a hotelier and assistant manager in a Tour Operator Agency. Her experience at DCMA has led her to believe in the need to revitalize the arts and cultural sector in Zanzibar, giving it a local perspective and vision. She lives in Zanzibar, is married, and has three children.

Keyna Eleison is a curator, researcher, and educator in art and culture. Eleison coordinated all public institutions from the Rio de Janeiro Municipal Department of Culture and taught at the Escola de Artes Visuais do Parque Lage, where she was also a teaching coordinator. She was the curator of the 10th Bienal Internacional de SIART in Bolivia (2018), the curator of the 1st Bienal das Amazônias (2023), the artistic director of the MAM Rio (2020-2023) and director of research and content at the Bienal das Amazônias.

Khamis Muhamed Juma is an artist, curator, and cultural advocate from Zanzibar. With over three decades of experience in fine arts, cultural management, and community development, he has dedicated his career to preserving and promoting African and Swahili art forms through education, exhibitions, and creative projects.

Mohamed Ameir Muombwa is an accomplished media professional, government advisor, and social development advocate with a career spanning over three decades in public service and journalism. His extensive experience in government, media relations, and community development has positioned him as a key figure in promoting Zanzibar's cultural and political narrative.

Mohamed Ilyas is one of Zanzibar's most iconic Taarab musicians, known for preserving and enriching the islands' cultural heritage. His music blends the Arabic roots of Taarab with a distinctly Zanzibari style, often incorporating European-inspired melodies into his songs.

Rukia Ramadhani is a celebrated Zanzibari singer and musician whose journey into the world of Taraab music reflects her lifelong passion and dedication to the art form.

Siti Muharam
See pp. 46-47.

Tanka Fonta is a visual artist, poet, writer, composer, and philosopher. His work explores human consciousness, the psychology of perception, and the interplay between thought, language, and visual phenomena. Fonta's practice investigates the expressive and perceptual dimensions of thought, the evolving ecologies of the mind, and the mytho-poetic narratives that shape human experience. He has participated in exhibitions at institutions such as Haus der Kulturen der Welt and SAVVY Contemporary, in Berlin, and Kunstverein Hannover.

Thabit Omar Kiringe is a highly respected music educator and one of the founders of the Dhow Countries Music Academy (DCMA). His contributions to music education and the preservation of traditional Taarab music are widely celebrated.

Thania Petersen is a multi-disciplinary artist who uses photography, performance and installation to address the intricacies and complexities of her identity in contemporary South Africa. Petersen's reference points sit largely in Islam and in creating awareness about its religious, cultural and traditional practices. She attempts to unpack contemporary trends of Islamophobia through her analysis of the continuing impact of colonialism, European and American imperialism, and the increasing influence of right-wing ideologies.

Tryphon Evarist is a musician, composer, traditional dancer, and teacher from Zanzibar, Tanzania, where he serves as the Artistic Director of the Dhow Countries Music Academy. Tryphon has mastered a diverse array of musical instruments, including the accordion, clarinet, qanun, and traditional drums, with a commitment to preserving African cultural arts.

Uwaridi Female Band
See pp. 44-45.

Thiago de Paula Souza is a curator and educator. He was co-curator of the 38th Panorama of Brazilian Art at MAM São Paulo (2024), the exhibition *Some May Work as Symbols: Art Made in Brazil, 1950s–70s* at Raven Row (London), the Nomadic Program at Vleeshal Center for Contemporary Art (Middelburg) between 2022 and 2023, *While We Are Embattled*, at Para Site, Hong Kong), and *Atos de Revolta* (MAM Rio) in 2022. Between 2020 and 2021, he was part of the curatorial team for the 3rd edition of *Frestas – Trienal de Artes* (São Paulo). He served as curatorial advisor for the 58th Carnegie International (2021-2022). From 2018 to 2019, he curated Tony Cokes' first solo exhibition at BAK (Utrecht). He was also part of the curatorial team of the 10th Berlin Biennale (2018). He is currently a member of the Artistic Committee of the NESR Art Foundation in Angola and is a PhD candidate in the arts program at HDK-Valand – University of Gothenburg.

advisors
André Leitão
Renato Lopes
Tailicie Nascimento
assistants
Gabri Gregorio
Giovanna Endrigo
Julia Iwanaga
Vinicius Massimino
apprentice
Lincon Amaral

Bienal Archive
manager
Leno Veras
coordinators
Antonio Paulo Carretta
Marcele Souto Yakabi
assistants
Ana Helena Grizotto Custódio
Anna Beatriz Corrêa Bortoletto
Daniel Malva Ribeiro
Gislene Sales
Gustavo Paes
Kleber Costa Timoteo
Raquel Coelho Moliterno
Thais Ferreira Dias
apprentices
Ilana Alionço
Manoel Assis

Financial and Administrative
Finances
manager
Amarildo Firmino Gomes
coordinator
Edson Pereira de Carvalho
advisor
Fábio Kato
assistant
Silvia Andrade Simões Branco

Materials and Property
manager
Valdomiro Rodrigues da Silva Neto
coordinators
Larissa Di Ciero Ferradas · *materials
and property*
Vinícius Robson da Silva Araújo ·
purchasing
assistants
Angélica de Oliveira Divino
Daniel Pereira
Sergio Faria Lima
Victor Senciel
Wagner Pereira de Andrade
auxiliary
Isabela Cardoso
apprentice
Lucas Galhardo

Planning and Operations
advisors
Rone Amabile
Vera Lucia Kogan

Human Resources
coordinators
Andréa Moreira · *human resources*
Higor Tocchio · *payroll and
personnel department*
assistants
Matheus Andrade Sartori
Patricia Fernandes

Information Technology
consultants
Ricardo Bellucci
Júlio Coelho
Matheus Lourenço
assistant
Jhones Alves do Nascimento

**36ª Bienal de São Paulo –
*Not All Travellers Walk Roads
– Of Humanity as Practice***

Conceptual Team
Bonaventure Soh Bejeng Ndikung ·
 chief curator
Alya Sebti, Anna Roberta Goetz,
 Thiago de Paula Souza · *co-curators*
Keyna Eleison · *co-curator at large*
Henriette Gallus · *strategy and
communications advisor*
André Pitol, Leonardo Matsuhei ·
curatorial assistants

Architecture and Exhibition
Design
Gisele de Paula, Tiago Guimarães
Alexandra Souza, Santiago Rid ·
 architectural assistance
Agence Clémence Farrell ·
 initial architectural advisory

Visual Identity
Studio Yukiko

Projects and Production
Acoustic Advisory
Alexandre Sresnewsky

Assembly Coordination
Alexandre Cruz
Arão Nunes
Mauro Amorim

Audiovisual Advisory
Patrícia Mesquita

Conservation
coordination
Patrícia Guimarães dos Reis

team
Alice Quintella Tischer
Daniel Zuim Mussi
Ellen Marianne Röpke Ferrando
Fabiana Franco Barbosa Oda
Gisele Guedes
Thaís Ramos Carvalhais
Valerie Midori Koga Takeda

Fine Arts Insurance
Sonia Sassi

Public Program Production
Helena Prado

Transportation Logistcs
Nilson Lopes · *national*
Waiver Arts · *international*

Communications and Editorial
AV Content and Photographic
Documentation
Bruno Fernandes
Duma Hub de Inovação Criativa e
 Produção Artística
João Gabriel Hidalgo

Design Assistance
Aninha de Carvalho Price
Tamara Lichtenstein

Editorial
Cristina Fino · *editorial
 coordination of the educational
 publications #3 / #4*
Deborah Moreira · *editorial
 assistance*

Press Office
Index · *national press office*
Sam Talbot · *international press office*

Invocations

Marrakech – Nov 14-15, 2024
LE 18 · *co-convener*
Laila Hida · *partner venue direction*
Youssef Sebti · *local production*
Zora El Hajji · *local press office*
Mahacine Mokdad, Sofian Amly,
 Hamza Morchid, Youssef
 Boumbarek · *AV content and
 photographic documentation*
Embaixada do Brasil em Rabat /
 Instituto Guimarães Rosa ·
 Ministério das Relações
 Exteriores – *local support*

Guadeloupe – Dec 5-7, 2024
Lafabri'K · *co-convener*
Marie-Laure Poitout · *partner venue
 presidency*
Léna Blou · *partner venue direction*
Hellen Rugard · *local production*
Annik Benjamin · *simultaneous
 translation*
Cédric Marcellin, Philippe Hurgon –
 *AV content and photographic
 documentation*
Institut Français; Embaixada do
 Brasil em Paris / Instituto
 Guimarães Rosa · Ministério das
 Relações Exteriores · *local support*

Zanzibar – Feb 11-13, 2025
Bernard Ntahondi · *co-convener*
Dhow Countries Music Academy
 (DCMA) · *partner institution*
Halda Alkanaan · *partner
 institution direction*

Thureiya Saleh · *local production*
Raymond Peter, Alex Marcel –
 sound engineering
William Chazega Nkobi,
 Habibu Ramadhani Diliwa · *simul-
 taneous translation*
Aden Rajab Said, Ally Nassor, Arafat
 Khamis Moh'd, Caroline-Jamie
 Dandu, Gulaam Abdullah, Venance
 Leonard, Waleed Khamis
 Mohammed · *AV content and
 photographic documentation*
YAS, Fondation H, Embaixada do
 Brasil em Dar es Salaam / Instituto
 Guimarães Rosa · Ministério das
 Relações Exteriores · *local support*

Tokyo – Apr 12-14, 2025
Andrew Maerkle, Kanako
 Sugiyama – *co-convener*
The 5th Floor; Sogetsu Kaikan;
 The University of Tokyo (with
 ACUT) · *venues*
Jordan A. Y. Smith · *poetry program
 advising*
Tomoya Iwata · *local production*
Yoshiko Kurata · *local press office*
Wataru Shoji · *sound engineering*
Art Translators Collective · *simulta-
 neous translation*
Kenji Agata, Naoki Takehisa, Sora
 Shirai, Takuma Osugi, Yoshikatsu
 Hirayama · *AV content and photo-
 graphic documentation*
Embaixada do Brasil em Tóquio /
 Instituto Guimarães Rosa ·
 Ministério das Relações Exteriores;
 Art Center, The University of
 Tokyo (ACUT) · *local support*

Educational Publication #3

Edited by
Conceptual team and Fundação
 Bienal de São Paulo

Published by
Fundação Bienal de São Paulo and
 Center for Art, Research and
 Alliances (CARA), in Portuguese
 and English

Design
Studio Yukiko

Editorial coordination and
Cristina Fino

Graphic production and layout
Fundação Bienal de São Paulo

Editorial assistance
Deborah Moreira

Copyediting and proofreading
Bruno Rodrigues, Mariana Nacif
 Mendes, Richard Sanches,
 Sandra Brazil

Translation
Alexandre Barbosa de Souza,
 Bruna Barros & Jess Oliveira,
 Jéssica Alonso, Philip Somervell

Font families
Arizona and Camera Plain
 by Dinamo

Printing
Ipsis

ISBN
978-1-954939-13-4

Distributed worldwide by
ARTBOOK | D.A.P.
75 Broad Street, Suite 630
New York, NY 10004
orders@dapinc.com
www.artbook.com

The title of the 36th Bienal de São
Paulo, *'Not All Travellers Walk
Roads'*, is made up of verses by the
writer Conceição Evaristo

Fundação Bienal de São Paulo
Av. Pedro Álvares Cabral – Moema
04094-050 / São Paulo – SP
bienal.org.br

Center for Art, Research and Alliances (CARA)
225 West 13th Street
New York, NY 10011
cara-nyc.org

Cataloging in Publication (CIP)

Mawali—Taqsim: Improvisation as a Space and Technology of Humanity
    educational publication: vol. 3 /
    edited by Fundação Bienal de São Paulo;
    curated by Bonaventure Soh Bejeng Ndikung. -- São Paulo:
    Fundação Bienal de São Paulo, 2025.

ISBN 978-1-954939-13-4

1. Art – São Paulo (State) – Exhibitions
2. Bienal de São Paulo (SP)
3. Culture
4. Education
5. Mediation

I. Fundação Bienal de São Paulo.
II. Ndikung, Bonaventure Soh Bejeng.

25-273124   CDD-709.8161

Systematic Catalog Index:
Art Biennials: São Paulo: City 709.8161

Marcele Souto – Librarian – CRB-8/9241

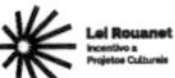 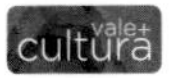 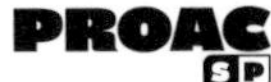

---

strategic partnership

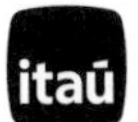

---

master sponsorship

Bloomberg bradesco **BR PETROBRAS** VALE citi vivo

sponsorship

---

motiva Alupar ROLEX ultra [B]³

Lhoist OSKLEN CSN CHANDON comgas

MATTOS FILHO UBS IGUATEMI SÃO PAULO Klabin ROSEWOOD SÃO PAULO Unipar

J.Macêdo OliverWyman AGEO COMOLATTI AUTOMOB

sabesp BANCO ABC BRASIL VERDE asset management união biolab FARMACÊUTICA

support

IOCHPE-MAXION Toledo do Brasil Indústria de Balanças Ltda BR.PARTNERS Banco Safra Racional

PINHEIRO NETO ADVOGADOS Instituto Rodobens CHOCOLAT DU JOUR instituto VOTORANTIM BAHIA ASSET MANAGEMENT J.P.Morgan

| official carrier | official agency | midia support | | | | cultural partnership |

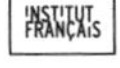 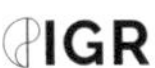 Creative 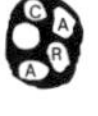 arte1 INSTITUTO BANDEIRANTES AQA C& AMÉRICA LATINA Sesc

international support

INSTITUT FRANÇAIS IGR GARA AaL BERG FOUNDATION TAF Tanoto Art Foundation National Center for Art Research, Japan

local support

OCA Office for Contemporary Art Norway yas Canada Council Conseil des arts for the Arts du Canada ARTS COUNCIL NEW ZEALAND TOI AOTEAROA creative nz FONDATION H EMBASSY OF BRAZIL DAR ES SALAAM

| institutional support | realization |

 SP CIDADE DE TODAS AS ARTES 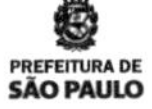 PREFEITURA DE SÃO PAULO 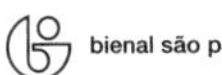 bienal são paulo CULT SP SP SÃO PAULO GOVERNO DO ESTADO SÃO PAULO SÃO TODOS Secretaria da Cultura, Economia e Indústria Criativas MINISTÉRIO DAS RELAÇÕES EXTERIORES MINISTÉRIO DA CULTURA GOVERNO FEDERAL BRASIL UNIÃO E RECONSTRUÇÃO